BILLY THE KID RIDES AGAIN

Praise for
Billy the Kid Rides Again

"Bravo! Excelsior!! By asking all the right questions and putting his conclusions where they counted, Jay Miller gave heart to those who, alone, would have been unable to combat such devious chicanery."

–Frederick Nolan, Chalfont St. Giles, England,
Author of "The West of Billy the Kid"

"In a series of newspaper columns, Jay Miller has dug deeply into the latest exploitation of Billy the Kid. A book packed with top-notch investigative reporting."

–Robert M. Utley, Georgetown, Texas,
Author of "Billy the Kid: a Short and Violent Life"

"Miller systematically demolished the baloney behind the campaign for exhumation. For a long time he was as much a lone gunman as Billy the Kid ever was."

–David A. Clary, Roswell, New Mexico,
Author of "Rocket Man: Robert Goddard
and the Birth of he Space Age"

"Anyone interested in learning about New Mexico should first check with Jay Miller. This collection of Jay's columns is the first in a series of books about New Mexico history and current events. It's a must read."

–Bill Richardson, Governor of New Mexico

BILLY THE KID RIDES AGAIN

Digging for the Truth

Jay Miller

SUNSTONE PRESS

SANTA FE

The opinions and ideas expressed in this book
are not necessarily those of the publisher.

Sunstone books may be purchased for educational, business, or sales
promotional use. For information please write: Special Markets Department,
Sunstone Press, P.O. Box 2321, Santa Fe, New Mexico 87504-2321.

Library of Congress Cataloging-in-Publication Data:

Miller, Jay, 1938-
  Billy the Kid rides again : digging for the truth / by Jay Miller.
    p. cm.
  ISBN 0-86534-458-2 (softcover : alk. paper)
1. Billy, the Kid-Death and burial. 2. Roberts, William Henry, 1859-1950.
3. Outlaws-Southwest, New-Biography. 4. Impostors and imposture-
United States. 5. Exhumation-New Mexico-Fort Sumner. 6. DNA finger-
printing-New Mexico-Fort Sumner. I. Title.

F786.B54M55 2005
364.15'52092-dc22

                                    2005026939

Published in
Santa Fe

WWW.SUNSTONEPRESS.COM
SUNSTONE PRESS / POST OFFICE BOX 2321 / SANTA FE, NM 87504-2321 /USA
(505) 988-4418 / ORDERS ONLY (800) 243-5644 / FAX (505) 988-1025

This book is dedicated to my wife Jeanette,
who cheerfully, although I suspect not willingly,
endured the partial loss of a husband
to months of investigative reporting.

CONTENTS

ACKNOWLEDGEMENTS

My interest in Billy the Kid and Pat Garrett began at an early age when my grandmothers, Laura Smith Miller and Annis Ford Meyer, of Las Cruces, New Mexico told me stories of Billy and Pat. They both were friendly with the Garrett family, who lived just down the street from the Meyers. And the Garrett family plot lies close to the Millers' in the Las Cruces Masonic Cemetery. In addition, I spent my high school years in Silver City, New Mexico, hearing tales of young Billy's adventures in the community and of his mother's gravesite being located somewhere in town.

Thus my fascination with this chapter in the lives of both men. As I wrote about the exciting events, I realized I was going to need the help of experts to answer questions I had about the way this story was unfolding. My friend Dave Clary, a Roswell historian with expertise in what seems like everything, led me to Robert Utley in Texas, and soon I made contact with Frederick Nolan in England and Leon Metz in El Paso.

Blessed with these contacts with the premier Billy the Kid, Pat Garrett and Lincoln County War scholars in the world, I was able to attack the impressive-looking Probable Cause Statement from the district court filing for Catherine Antrim's exhumation in Silver City. Their analysis meant my suspicions were confirmed that there was more to this case than met the eye.

I then began an effort to determine what public money was being spent on this case and how it was being spent. My thanks go to Robert Johnson of the Foundation for Open Government for his help in guiding me through the quest. Thank you also to De Baca County Clerk Nancy Sparks for her quick and helpful responses.

When I bogged down in the forensics of finding DNA, blood and bullet holes, I received willing assistance from some of the most respected forensic scientists in the nation, among them Tom Mauriello, Brian Wraxall, Dr. Clyde Snow and Dr. Edward Blake.

Helpful input came from Dr. Gale Cooper, a Harvard educated M.D. forensic psychiatrist, who had spent several years researching the history of the Lincoln County War, Billy the Kid and the Santa Fe Ring for a book she was writing. She used her expertise to identify the many inconsistencies in the Billy the Kid case and worked with others throughout New Mexico in its opposition.

Also helpful in providing background information were Fort Sumner Mayor Raymond Lopez, Lincoln County Commissioner Leo Martinez, Maryln Bolin, Rose Barton and Trish Saunders.

For the photographs in this book, I am indebted to Robert McCubbin, Bob Boze Bell of True West magazine and Joe Micalizzi, webmaster of www.BillytheKidsNewMexico.com.

New Mexico Governor Bill Richardson has been supportive of this effort and of my future plans for several additional books designed to promote New Mexico and New Mexicans. He realizes I was pretty tough on him in this collection of columns for staying on the grave-digging kick much longer than I thought he should. He maintains, however, that his only interest in Billy is to promote New Mexico.

This book would not have been possible without the three sheriffs, the villains of the story. It also wouldn't have been needed, because they're the ones who caused all the commotion. I know they thought my investigation was unnecessary. We may never know what caused them to pull out of the Fort Sumner court hearing, but I figure my attempt to shed more light on the subject may have had something to do with it. To the extent their efforts end up aiding tourism in Billy the Kid Country, I applaud them.

Since this is the first of what I hope to be many books that will pull together some of my 6,000 columns on several subjects that have been of special interest to me, I want to thank the patient editors and publishers who helped guide me through the early years of this my second career, for which I had no formal training.

For whatever writing skills I might possess, I have only to thank my Deming Junior High English teacher, Joe Stell, now a state representative from Carlsbad and Stella Vaughan, my high school English teacher in Silver City. I have always wanted to thank them. Since this now sounds suspiciously like an Oscar acceptance speech, I will mercifully end.

–Jay Miller

FOREWORD

One of the great showman P. T. Barnum's most popular exhibits in his museum of the bizarre a century and a half ago was the "Feejee Mermaid." It was a clumsy taxidermical monstrosity involving the half-corpses of a monkey and a fish, presented as an authentic mermaid from the far Pacific. It was a patent fraud, yet thousands of people paid their nickels just to look at it, inspiring Barnum's most famous utterance, "There's a sucker born every minute."

Americans, it appears, have always had an insatiable appetite for trashistory and pseudoscience, for nonsense presented as fact. An interesting part of this phenomenon has been the claim that this or that corpse was not in fact dead, but that somebody else was the "real" living legend. Objects of such fantasies go back to the earliest part of our history. They have included such figures as Indian leaders Tecumseh and Cochise, foreign soldiers such as Marshal Ney (an interesting case there-at least two people claimed to be Ney during the 1820s, while the real Ney was living under an assumed name in South Carolina), Abraham Lincoln and his killer John Wilkes Booth, and so on up to John F. Kennedy and his killer Lee Harvey Oswald. And let us not forget other characters from Russian Princess Anastasia to German Nazi Martin Bormann to singer Elvis Presley.

Criminals have not escaped this phenomenon. In the 20th century a legion of imposters claimed to be the "real" Jesse

James, or Butch Cassidy–or Billy the Kid. If these stories have a common attribute, it is that they are all based on assertions utterly devoid of fact. As such, they belong on the trash heap with allegations that the government is covering up the truth about space aliens, or that the (insert your favorite shadowy group here) engineered the assassination of President Kennedy. Yet those yarns also persist.

Case in point–the fight for Billy's Bones. In 1881 Pat Garrett shot Billy the Kid to death in Ft. Sumner, New Mexico. Acquaintances identified the body as Billy's. A corner's jury examined the corpse and circumstances and declared the outlaw's demise to be justifiable homicide by Garrett in the performance of his duty. The departed was duly installed in the local graveyard. Billy, not surprisingly, was never seen or heard from again. Case closed, right?

Not in America, where fact can be a malleable substance. In the 20th century several old fellows, of whom the best known was "Brushy Bill" Roberts of Hico, Texas, popped up claiming to be the "real" Billy the Kid. In each case there was a conspiratorial explanation of how somebody else ended up in the famous outlaw's grave. No facts supported these claims, and what facts did exist contradicted them–besides the legal record in Billy's case, Brushy Bill's own family records revealed that he was a small child when the Kid rode the range. But like the Feejee Mermaid, Brushy Bill gained a gullible audience, unsuccessfully petitioned the governor of New Mexico for a pardon, then went to his own grave in 1952.

A half-century later, two New Mexico county sheriffs, evidently not having enough modern crime to contend with, decided to reopen the case of Billy's death. They aimed to find out what "really happened" in 1881, hang the historical and legal record, using Brushy Bill as a starting point. Their exercise in trashistory became an obsession, and reached out into pseudoscience with a campaign to dig up whatever remained of Billy and later his mother, in hopes of finding DNA. They apparently believed that chemical to be some spirit of the past that would tell its tale and give them fifteen minutes on television.

As if this theater of the absurd was not silly enough, the state's governor got into the act. He appointed an attorney to speak for Billy in court. Via this medium, Billy told the judge he wanted to be dug up, and his mama along with him. Residents of the two communities where the graves are located, Fort. Sumner and Silver City, were appalled at the impending desecration of their historic sites. But how could they overcome the political and legal firepower ranged against them?

As a historian, and a historian of science at that, I believe that arguments should be based on fact. Here was a case where not only were there no historical facts that would justify violating two graves, but science also was being abused. DNA, in the unlikely event that it could be retrieved, which depended on the unlikely event that any remains could be identified with Billy or his mama, is not magic. It is chemistry, and it has its uses, but it is not an all-revealing oracle. When, I wondered, would somebody speak out against this malarkey, this abuse of the taxpayers' money in the service of trashistory and pseudoscience?

Somebody did. Santa Fe columnist Jay Miller, in a series of increasingly pointed columns, raised one after another issues of fact, history and science, and of propriety. For a long time his fight was a lonely one. Absurd as it sounds, there were rumors of retaliation by various offended parties, including the sheriffs and the governor, and even of death at the hands of Brushy Bill's partisans. Ignoring all that, Jay soldiered on. He systematically demolished the baloney behind the campaign for exhumation, and exposed the abuses of office that accompanied the whole business. In the end, when the critical case was tossed out of court, Jay Miller won a sterling victory for Truth over the champions of nonsense.

This book brings together Jay's columns and other material, so that readers can relive one man's quest for honesty where history, science, and the public purse are concerned. I trust you will find it as entertaining and inspiring as I did. Jay observes that he had many supporters and helpers, but in all honesty he carried the fight on his own, as much a lone gunman as Billy the Kid ever was. This time, nobody was shot, and Jay demonstrated anew that the pen is mightier than sword or pistol.

–David A. Clary

INTRODUCTION

In early 2003, three sheriffs decided to reopen the Billy the Kid legend. Their reasons were confusing and their actions were random, all of which made their motives suspicious.

Were they in it to promote tourism? Were they looking for money and fame? Were they fronting for someone else with secret motives? Or were they, as they sometime said, three guys out to have some fun? Maybe it was a combination of all these.

They also said they were digging for the truth. But those truths kept changing. They wanted to prove that Pat Garrett shot Billy. They wanted to prove that Billy's pretenders were impostors, yet they spent much time trying to create doubt about who Garrett shot.

They wanted to find out what happened at the Lincoln County Courthouse when Billy escaped and two deputies were shot. And they left open the possibility that Garrett might have had something to do with Billy getting the gun with which he shot the first deputy. And sometimes they were helping Governor Bill Richardson decide whether to pardon Billy.

They acquired furniture they claim was in Pete Maxwell's room, where Garrett supposedly shot Billy. And then, for some mysterious reason, they shot up the antique furniture to see what happened.

Their random actions appear to reveal that these were three guys out on a lark, trying to add their names to a chapter of Billy's life.

The chapters in this book, each were a newspaper column, written between May 2003 and October 2004. They are in sequential order, giving a picture of how the story unfolded. The columns appeared in numerous newspapers throughout New Mexico. Minor changes have been made to a few of the columns to improve on clarity or accuracy. Otherwise you are experiencing the events as they unfolded.

Shoulder patch—Lincoln County Sheriff's Office. Depicting former Lincoln County Sheriff, Pat Garrett and Old Lincoln County Courthouse.

1

REOPENING THE KID'S CASE

(Published June 13, 2003)

Reopening the case of Billy the Kid may turn out to be as controversial as the Lincoln County War, in which the Kid gained his fame.

Longtime Lincoln County Sheriff Tom Sullivan and Steve Sederwall, identified as "a reserve officer for the sheriff's office," have asked Governor Bill Richardson for State Police assistance in getting to the bottom of the Billy the Kid legend. They have also involved Dale Tunnell, a special investigator for the Arizona Department of Corrections.

A mention of the investigation a few weeks ago in this column has brought accusatory letters from readers in Lincoln County about everybody concerned with the case. Evidently the investigation is opening some old wounds and some more current ones.

Teachers in schools around Lincoln, which was the center of the Lincoln County War, have said that bitter feelings about the war still erupt on playgrounds among descendents of families that have been in the area since the war began in the early 1880s. It's like taking sides on whether Oliver Lee of Alamogordo shot Albert Jennings Fountain of Las Cruces back in the 1890s.

And there are animosities of a more current nature. Sederwall not only is a deputy sheriff, he is mayor of nearby Capitan. Evidently he has a few political enemies here and there who question his motives for encouraging the investigation.

Tunnell and Sederwall are old law enforcement buddies from the Lincoln County sheriff's office, who are teaming for this investigation. I've also heard from those who say Governor Richardson is only cooperating in the investigation so he can get his face plastered all over the nation's newspapers.

For the record, Sullivan and Sederwall say they want to unearth the truth about Billy's escape from the Lincoln County jail and about whether he was the one Sheriff Pat Garret shot. At least five other people claimed to be Billy and told varying stories about how Garrett had shot someone else and claimed it was the Kid.

Sullivan says that accusation reflects on the Lincoln County sheriff's office, which has made Garrett very much a part of its history, including making him a part of their shoulder patches. They want to clear his name. Sullivan says opening the investigation has nothing to do with increasing tourism in the area.

But what if it is a reason for the investigation? Tourism is a major part of the area's economy, which could use some help. The historic, but financially struggling, Wortley Hotel, across the street from the old Lincoln County Courthouse, from which Billy escaped, might no longer be on the edge of closing down.

Billy the Kid is still New Mexico's most recognizable figure. I've never seen research on this, but Smokey Bear, also from Lincoln County, may be second. Sullivan says the investigation won't cost the county anything, since Sederwall is a volunteer.

If Richardson authorizes State Police assistance, there will be some cost. Richardson says this isn't a publicity stunt. It's an integral part of New Mexico's past and if it is possible to shed new light on the legend, we should.

Certainly there may be personal motives tied to the investigation. It is a fascinating project for a retired cop, who might get some publicity out of the venture. Governor Richardson may be looking at the publicity angle too but more likely he wants publicity for the state as part of his effort to put us on the map.

The investigation may have side benefits. Several books have been written, some by New Mexicans, about the possibility Billy lived a long life. They may see a resurgence. Various claimed burial sites will also see a renewed interest, including the burial site of Billy's mother in Silver City.

2

DISAPPOINTING DNA

(Published July 25, 2003)

New Mexico's plan to use DNA testing on Billy the Kid and various wannabes is fraught with dangers that likely will disappoint the tourism industry.

Not that New Mexico needs to worry about any of the other claimants in Texas or Arizona turning out to be the real Billy, it's just that DNA testing of remains over 120 years old is difficult and expensive, not to mention the uncertainty of whether the remains even belong to the right person.

Southwestern cemeteries in the 1870s and 1880s, when Billy and his mother were buried, weren't secure. Soon after Billy was buried in Fort Sumner, stories of grave robbers stealing his remains already were circulating. If those stories were half as accurate as the number of times his grave marker is known to have been stolen, Billy may not be anywhere close to Fort Sumner.

Then there's the problem with two pals, Charlie Bowdre and Tom O'Folliard, being buried in the same grave, if we are to believe his current tombstone. That means a lot of remains will have to be tested.

And we can't be sure it is the right grave. In those days graves were marked by wooden crosses and no reliable records of grave sites were kept. In the early 1900s, the Pecos River flooded and washed away many markers and possibly some bodies. By the time a permanent marker was erected in the 1930s, it would have been very difficult to estimate the exact burial sites.

The location of Billy's mother's grave in Silver City also carries some questions. She was transferred from her original burial site to Memory Lane Cemetery in 1882, along with a number of other bodies. We can't be certain the land developer doing the transferring got everything right.

Exhumations involve legal processes, so authorities in Fort Sumner and Silver City will have to give their approval. Silver City has never made a big deal out of Catherine Antrim's grave site but Billy's grave in Fort Sumner is a big attraction. It now is generally accepted as being authentic. What will happen if no DNA from that grave site matches DNA from the Silver City site? How do we explain that? Might it be better to leave well-enough alone?

Although reopening the kid's case has its detractors, there is no denying that it can be good for tourism if handled correctly. Ideally that means forgetting about the DNA stuff but we're probably into that to far already. Governor Bill Richardson has pledged state help and has asked for assistance from our two national labs. If the results aren't good, the governor's spinmeisters will have to find a way to dance around them.

Governor Richardson says he plans to appoint a defense counsel and prosecutor to present evidence at hearings in Silver City, Mesilla, Fort Sumner and Lincoln, all of which played a major part in Billy's life.

Billy grew up in Silver City and is said by some to have shot his first man there for making unwanted advances on his mother. The trial in which he was convicted of killing Lincoln County Sheriff William Brady was held in Mesilla. Lincoln was the center of the Lincoln County War. And Fort Sumner was where Sheriff Pat Garrett tracked down Billy and shot him.

Hearings in these four locations would be sure to attract international attention because of worldwide fascination with the story. They wouldn't likely unearth any new facts but they could serve to educate all of us about the Kid's life and straighten out many misconceptions.

And our governor has found a way to tie himself into the action. Billy shot the two deputies after New Mexico's most famous governor, Lew Wallace, couldn't deliver on his promise to pardon the Kid in return for Billy testifying to what he knew about one of the many murders in the Lincoln County War.

"I feel a certain responsibility if Lew Wallace made such a promise," Richardson says.

Billy's celebrity status resulted in so many thefts of his tombstone that a cage had to built around his gravesite.

3

INTERNATIONAL HERO

(Published August 24, 2003)

As predicted, right here in this column, reopening the Billy the Kid case has created worldwide interest–and controversy.

In every country where western movies are popular, and that's just about everywhere, people know about Billy. It is claimed that Hollywood has made more movies about the Kid than any other historical character.

Actors including Paul Newman, Audie Murphy, Buster Crabbe, Roy Rogers, Kris Kristofferson and Emilio Estevez have portrayed the guy in movies dating back to 1911. Many strayed far from historical fact, such as the 1966 flick Billy the Kid Versus Dracula, but the name, by itself, is a grabber.

What makes Billy the Kid such a compelling character? Maybe it's the fact he was young, good at what he did, wasn't getting rich from it and was a victim of the circumstances in which he grew up. People evidently see more good in him than bad.

His first victim was purportedly a traveling salesman who got fresh with his mother, a waitress in a Silver City eatery. He worked for the side in the Lincoln County war that is portrayed as the good guys. And he survived an amazingly long time considering the odds. His life was ended only by someone who may have shot him from ambush.

The end of Billy's life was surrounded by enough ambiguity to foster many tales of conspiracy. According to some accounts, the body was buried before a coroner's jury arrived and all it could do was take statements from Sheriff Pat Garrett.

Since Garrett and the Kid were supposedly close, that has led to many stories about Garrett killing someone else and letting Billy and his Spanish girlfriend escape. Thus, all the stories about Billy's long life in Texas or Arizona.

The folks in Hico, Texas have been making much noise lately about their guy, Brushy Bill, being the real Kid despite all evidence pointing otherwise. His family bible lists Brushy as being born two years before Billy died. The Kid was a young gun, but not that young.

These are the same Texans who claim Jesse James died of old age in those parts, along with John Wilkes Booth, who evidently gave up his acting career to be a bartender. Guess we should feel sorry for the fellow having to stand up all night on that broken leg.

The Texans like New Mexico's idea of DNA testing, except that they don't want any of it done on their guy. "If they've been telling the truth for 120 years about the gravesite," says one, "why would they need to come to Texas?"

Our Governor's Office doesn't think much of that idea. It wants to test Catherine Antrim, who is buried in Silver City, and then test the claimants in Texas and Arizona. The folks in Fort Sumner are adamant about not digging up Billy's grave there. The granddaughter of the Chamber of Commerce director says she will chain herself to the fence surrounding the grave if anyone starts digging.

So while both sides want only to prove the negative, the DNA talk continues. But it really won't go anywhere. Graves can't just be dug up. Court orders are necessary. And if the local folks don't want it, it's not going to happen.

It seems likely that everyone has a pretty good idea that no DNA matches will be found. Both Catherine's and Billy's graves have been moved and even if their remains could be found, it is unlikely they would produce enough to work with after 120 years. The bones of Jesse James were exhumed a few years ago and the findings were inconclusive.

As noted historian Robert Utley observes, "Something this far in the past is not a fit subject for police methods, only for historical methods."

And Governor Bill Richardson has that covered. He plans to appoint a defense counsel and a prosecutor to present evidence at hearings in Silver City, Mesilla, Fort Sumner and Lincoln, all places where major events in Billy's life occurred.

4

THE SEARCH FOR BILLY'S BONES

(Published November 3, 2003)

The search for Billy's bones has begun. The sheriffs' offices in Lincoln and DeBaca counties have filed a petition asking the Grant County District Court to order exhumation of the body of Catherine Antrim, Billy the Kid's mother.

This exhumation may be easier than previous efforts to dig up the remains of Billy and other celebrities because this one is being done as part of a reopened investigation of the Kid's death, 122 years ago.

Sherry Tippett, an attorney representing Lincoln and DeBaca county authorities says the normal procedure is to get a permit for exhumation from the state medical investigator's office. But Tippett says she and the sheriffs decided to go to District Court for an order so the process will be open and any complaints can be heard.

And there will be complaints. The mayors of Silver City and Fort Sumner both have announced their opposition to unearthing Billy's mama's bones.

Tippett claims a forensic anthropologist from the state Office of the Medical Investigator says she has researched the burial history on the exact location of Antrim's remains and is confident they can be exhumed without disturbing other graves, according to the court petition.

That claim is subject to debate since the entire cemetery in which Antrim was buried was moved many years ago to make room for a housing development. If someone else's remains are unearthed, the DNA from those surely won't match whatever might be found in Billy's grave. That possibility naturally bothers Fort Sumner Mayor Raymond Lopez. The DNA testing, by the way, will be privately funded.

The Silver City mayor and some of his council members aren't pleased that no one has consulted with the town of Silver City. They see it as no more than a publicity stunt.

The sheriffs and Governor Bill Richardson are trying to untangle some of the historical questions surrounding the Kid's death. There have long been stories that Billy may not have been killed that night in Fort Sumner. Some say Sheriff Pat Garrett may have shot someone else and claimed it was Billy.

The coroner's jury, in its report to the New Mexico attorney general, attested that it viewed the body and unanimously agreed it was William Bonney, although stories persist that the jury didn't arrive until after the body was buried.

Governor Richardson says he wants a thorough analysis of what happened. His main interest seems to be the pardon that Governor Lew Wallace reportedly promised Billy in return for his telling all he knew about one of the murders in the Lincoln County War. Billy apparently upheld his end of the deal but wasn't let off as were others who testified. In fact, Billy was the only person convicted for any of the murders during the Lincoln County War.

According to accounts, that is what caused Billy to stage his daring escape from the Lincoln County Courthouse, killing two deputy sheriffs in the process. Evidently Governor Wallace wanted to deliver on his promise but the prosecutor wouldn't agree.

As recently as last January, purported descendants of The Kid have asked subsequent governors for that pardon, which has never been granted. Governor Richardson says he feels a certain responsibility to look into the matter and do the right thing. He also adds he wants the investigation to be right at all costs and not make any mistakes.

That's not easy 122 years later. But Richardson says he's going to appoint a prosecution and defense to argue the case in Silver City, Las Cruces, Lincoln and Fort Sumner. That obviously has its publicity and tourism value but the governor is playing with fire. He likes to be in control, but other people, with possibly other motives, also are involved.

DNA testing of hundred-year-old bodies will be inconclusive at best and prove nothing. A wave of crazies are bound to come out of the woodwork along with a spate of opportunists once the "investigation" gets rolling. And the whole thing may get out of control.

But it should be fun to watch.

5

BILLY GETS A LAWYER

(Published November 28, 2003)

Billy the Kid now has a defense counsel. Bill Robins, a history buff with law offices in Houston and Santa Fe, along with David Sandoval, have volunteered to represent Billy free of charge.

Why would anyone want to defend a dead outlaw pro bono, as they say in the biz? Robins speculates that "the whole world is following this story." If Robins' facts are correct, he may be on to something. Robins says Billy is our most famous New Mexican. That's a claim I've heard before, including from the mouths of people using it to run down our state. Guess not everyone is proud of having an outlaw as the state's most famous personality.

In fact, Robins says Billy's name is the second most recognizable in the world. A guy's in pretty tall cotton when the only person ahead of him is Elvis. One of author-singer Kinky Friedman's first books, was titled "Jesus, Elvis and Coca Cola." The three most recognizable elements of our culture in some obscure, third-world country Friedman was writing about. But he didn't mention Billy.

In our foreign travels over the years, we have run into more people who ask about Roswell, than about Billy when we mention we are from New Mexico. Maybe Roswell is more identified with New Mexico. Billy may mean mostly "Wild West" to foreigners.

But that could be changed with a good advertising campaign, and maybe that is what Governor Bill Richardson has in mind, with the hearings he wants conducted in Silver City, Las Cruces, Lincoln and Fort Sumner. If Billy the Kid really is second to Elvis as the most recognizable name in the world, New Mexico has a bright future ahead of it in the same league as Tennessee, with Graceland and all its surrounding businesses.

Of course, Billy never recorded any hits, but then neither did George Washington, who slept in enough places along the East Coast to keep dozens of bed and breakfasts open. With enough publicity, maybe the Wortley Hotel could open again in Lincoln.

I got zinged after writing last spring that the Wortley was closed. Its restaurant was open at the time but it closed a couple of months ago to the amazement of people in the area, because it seemed to always be packed.

A Billy the Kid Trail should be very successful with some publicity. Silver City has Billy's mother's grave and a fist full of stories about Billy's younger days. Some of the buildings tied to those stories are still standing.

Then there is Mesilla, where Billy hung out in his early years after leaving home. Some of those buildings still stand. Pat Garrett's grave has been moved to the Las Cruces Masonic Cemetery in the past few decades. And there are buildings in Mesilla tied to Albert Jennings Fountain, who defended Billy in his trial for killing Sheriff Brady.

In Lincoln, there is no shortage of Billy memorabilia, starting with the Courthouse, where he killed two deputies during his daring escape. Fort Sumner has his grave and a museum. Someone has spotted a big new gravestone in the White Oaks Cemetery on the grave of James W. Bell, one of the deputies Billy killed at the courthouse.

Las Vegas and Santa Fe also have sites associated with some of Billy's captures and incarcerations. A Santa Fe downtown business claims its basement is where Billy was held for several months, while attempting to get Governor Lew Wallace to grant his promised pardon.

That business has never advertised the fact, but probably should. And there are hangouts of the old Santa Fe Ring that controlled most of New Mexico at one time and took a big part in the Lincoln County War. Billy also spent some of his school days in Santa Fe.

Then there are Billy's various hideouts at Stinking Springs, El Ojo del Taiba and several other locations in south central New Mexico. He worked at many ranches around the state and made friends with numerous well-to-do ranchers, several of whom would give him and his friends a place to hole up, when needed. And he had girl friends spread all over the state.

6

BILLY SPEAKS

(Published December 28, 2003)

You'll be glad to know that Billy the Kid now has a voice. That was decided, on a temporary basis, by Henry Quintero, a district court judge in Silver City. And, as you might expect, Billy immediately began talking.

The essence of Billy's comments to the court, through his attorney Bill Robins, was that he supports the exhumation of his mother. The town of Silver City says it has the right to make that determination since it owns the cemetery where Catherine Antrim likely is buried. Billy says only heirs have the right to decide on an exhumation and he wants her dug up.

Judge Quintero has set a hearing on the matter for January 27 and will decide at that time whether Billy can participate and whether it is proper for Governor Bill Richardson to appoint a lawyer for him. Billy said the deceased always have in interest in what occurred to them.

Adam Baker, representing Silver City said a lawyer can't just walk into a court without a client and start presenting evidence. Billy said, watch what you're saying there, pardner.

Parties in this theater of the absurd are the petitioners, Capitan Mayor Steve Sederwall and Sheriffs Tom Sullivan and Gary Graves of Lincoln and DeBaca counties. They are represented by Sherry Tippett, a Silver City attorney, who formerly was an assistant Santa Fe city attorney and the first Green elected to the Santa Fe School Board. She also served a stint as attorney for Grant County

The petitioners want to dig up Catherine Antrim and take DNA samples to compare with people who claim to be Billy the Kid. They are running into a heap of trouble because none of the communities where bodies are allegedly buried want to turn over the remains.

Why shouldn't these communities want to cooperate with the interests of history and science? Silver City says because it is merely a publicity stunt. Fort Sumner, where Billy has a grave, agrees. Hico, Texas and Prescott, Arizona, where pretenders are claimed to be buried haven't been heard from, but are certain to oppose.

And they all likely are worried because of the high probability there won't be a DNA match. Even if Billy was shot by Pat Garrett and is buried in Fort Sumner, as history records, the DNA are unlikely to match because the passage of over 120 years destroys almost anything that can be tested. And the loss of Billy's gravestone and the movement of his mother's grave during that period lessens the possibility that bodies are exactly where they should be.

Judge Quintero allowed Silver City to intervene in the petition for exhumation because it is trustee of Memory Lane Cemetery, where Antrim is buried. The town also says it has an historical interest to protect. Tippett says that argument isn't valid because no attempt was made to give the grave historical designation before the petition for exhumation was entered.

All this fussing over grave robbing and DNA isn't likely to get anywhere. The judge has told attorneys for all sides that he still is troubled that there is no legitimate interest to be served by the exhumation and an investigation that will not lead to charges being filed against anyone.

Historian Dave Clary of Roswell suggests a much better solution than DNA matching to decide whether Brushy Bill in Hico, Texas was the real Billy. Handwriting analysis was successfully used in the case of a Jesse James pretender several years ago.

Billy the Kid wrote several letters from the Santa Fe jail to Governor Lew Wallace begging him to follow through with his promise for a pardon. Before his death in 1950, brushy Bill wrote letters to Governor Tom Mabry requesting him to issue the pardon Wallace never delivered on.

That correspondence to both Wallace and Mabry should be in the state archives and it would be much easier, cheaper and accurate than digging up bodies for old DNA.

7

THE WIDOW GARRETT SPEAKS

(Published January 23, 2004)

Is it weird enough for you yet? Well, the case of Billy the Kid has taken another step in the direction of the Twilight Zone.

When last we talked about Billy, a Silver City district judge had given him permission to speak through a lawyer appointed by Governor Bill Richardson. And Billy promptly told the judge he wanted his mother dug up from a local cemetery.

That might be a first in judicial history, but it certainly isn't the last. Now we have Pat Garrett's widow speaking from the grave to tell a 9-year-old boy that Pat really didn't kill Billy. We get this information from a sworn statement filed by a guy in California who says he was in Las Cruces once. Back in 19-aught-40, he visited a friend who just happened to live next door to Pat Garret's widow.

Mrs. Garrett invited the young boys over for tea one afternoon, and they accepted. Now that's mighty weird right there, folks. She told them that Pat and Billy found a drunk on the street in Fort Sumner, shot him up until he was unrecognizable and then put out the story it was Billy.

You might think it a bit weird for a 79-year-old woman to work a story like that into a conversation with two young boys, one of whom she has just met, over afternoon tea.

But that's really not the weird part. You see, she'd been dead for four years at the time. Somehow the California guy didn't include that in his statement. One would think it would have made a sufficient impression on him to have mentioned it in his affidavit, at least in passing.

That's the way it looks from up here in Santa Fe, anyway. A check of the New Mexico Index of Deaths on the Internet reveals that an Apolinoria G. Garrett died in Dona Ana County in 1936, at age 75.

The first name isn't spelled exactly as it appears elsewhere, but my crack research team feels rather confident that there probably weren't too many Garretts running around Las Cruces at the time with anything near that first name.

A check of the Internet also revealed that newspapers all over the country are carrying the Associated Press story about doubt being cast on whether Garrett really killed the kid. Maybe Billy, through his gubernatorially-appointed lawyer can explain this all to us at his next court appearance on Jan. 27, in Silver City.

While searching for Apolinaria (the preferred spelling by historians) Garrett in the Death Index, we also noticed that Pat Garrett's death was never recorded in New Mexico. Maybe he's buried over in Texas with Brushy Bill Roberts. After all, we have been told that they were good friends.

Wayne Brazel was arrested for killing Garrett, but attorney Albert Fall got him off. He's the same guy who successfully represented the two men charged with killing Albert Jennings Fountain. Maybe Fall's trick on this one was to see that Garrett's death wasn't recorded; therefore, he didn't officially die, so Brazel couldn't have killed him. Hey, weirder things have happened.

It also is amusing that another Brazel (Mac) was the person who, 40 years later, found the Roswell UFO, which was subsequently determined not to exist. Those Brazels were good at hiding the evidence.

Pat Garrett's grave does exist, although it has been moved. It now lies across the base of the Garrett family plot in the Masonic Cemetery in Las Cruces. But in light of recent findings, there could be some doubt that Garrett really is in it. The way things are going, someone is bound to want to dig it up too.

We're not through yet. My research team reports that lists of graves in the state of New Mexico do not show an Apolinaria G. Garrett, or any other spelling of her first name, to be buried anywhere in the state.

But historian John Wilson of Las Cruces sends me a photograph of her headstone right beside her husband.

8

LEGISLATURE CONSIDERS PARDON

(Published February 23, 2004)

A pardon for Billy the Kid was considered by the New Mexico Legislature at this time three years ago. The proposal took the time of only one committee before meeting a fate similar to that of the Kid and his victims. The measure was tabled and wasn't revived before its final death at session's end.

Media coverage was substantial. Numerous articles were generated when the measure was introduced. Many more appeared when the Tunstall family weighed in on Billy's behalf from England. More came when the committee took action. The Albuquerque Tribune carried a lengthy human-interest story on people in Fort Sumner whose families had told them stories about the Kid. That was followed by spirited pro and con essays in the editorial section.

Some of those stories went out of state on the wire and some made their way to the rest of the world where Wild West mania is a hot item and Billy is one of its biggest stars. So the small amount of legislative time spent was more than justified by the free tourism publicity.

Would a pardon for the Kid have dulled his tourism draw? Maybe so. Had Billy been pardoned in the first place, as

Governor Lew Wallace had promised, he probably would have faded into history alongside the other participants in the Lincoln County War.

It was the fact that Governor Wallace offered and issued pardons to the others involved in bloodshed but reneged on Billy's pardon that sparked the Kid's notoriety. It was while Billy was held in the Lincoln County jail awaiting execution for his part in the killing of Sheriff William Brady and a deputy that he escaped, killing two more deputies.

Wiping out four lawmen raises one's infamy to the level that a future life as a horse thief and cattle rustler is somewhat overlooked by history. Despite these crimes, Billy is viewed by many as a tragic figure because he fought on the side of the reputed good guy in the Lincoln County War.

John Tunstall came from England to make his fortune in the American West as a cattle rancher. Unfortunately he decided to do it in an area that was controlled by a rival interest with ties to the corrupt Santa Fe Ring. When the bad guys killed Tunstall, Brady and other law officers did nothing to bring the culprits to justice despite international diplomatic appeals by the well-connected Tunstall family.

So Billy took the law into his own hands, killing several of those who had been in on the Tunstall murder. Thus the current appeal from the Tunstall descendents for the Kid's pardon.

Billy's other support comes mainly from the Fort Sumner and Santa Rosa areas, where he had many Hispanic friends and, according to claims by Elbert Garcia, who requested the current pardon, fathered at least one child.

You don't find much sympathy for Billy in Lincoln, Dona Ana or Grant counties. The four lawmen Billy shot all worked for Lincoln County and it was Lincoln County Sheriff Pat Garrett who tracked the Kid to Fort Sumner and shot him, probably more for his rustling activity than for the lawmen he killed. Cattle barons, such as Charlie Goodnight, were putting on the pressure to rein him in.

Garrett later moved to Dona Ana County, where a local jury earlier had quickly convicted Billy of killing Sheriff Brady. The Kid had spent his early teen years in Grant County, where he was often in trouble. Many Silver City residents still consider him nothing more than a juvenile delinquent.

Feelings still run high in Billy's old stomping grounds about his reputation. Smart folks are careful about what they say in public lest they offend someone from the other persuasion.

The legend of Billy the Kid hasn't died, and for the sake of southern New Mexico tourism, that's a good thing.

9

DID BILLY HAVE A KID?

(Published March 19, 2004)

Add a new conspiracy theory to the Billy the Kid legend. We already have the mystery about where the gun came from that Billy found in the outhouse behind the Lincoln County Courthouse and which he used to kill the first of two deputy sheriffs. And we have the claim that Billy and Sheriff Pat Garrett conspired to kill someone else and claim it was Billy so he could leave town and start a new life.

Now a new program on the Discovery Channel claims that Garrett did shoot the Kid, from ambush, as he entered the bedroom of Paulita Maxwell, his pregnant girlfriend. Her parents had learned that she planned to run off with Billy that night and they wanted him stopped. After the shooting, they quickly got her married to someone else and six months later she bore a child who grew up to look very much like Billy.

It doesn't take a psychic to predict that soon pretenders will be coming out of the woodwork claiming to be great grandchildren of Billy. Using photographic analysis, the program did put down the claims that Brushy Bill Roberts, of Hico, Texas and John Miller, of Ramah, New Mexico and Prescott, Arizona were actually Billy. But it created a new legend about the bloodline of Billy the Kid.

And why not? That sort of story is selling quite well these days in a bestseller by Dan Brown, called The Da Vinci Code, in which Mary Magdalene marries Christ, bears his child, and flees to southern France and begins a dynasty of European kings imbued with divine rights. Maybe Brown can write about Billy's bloodline now. He spins a great yarn and people love a conspiracy.

A recent New York Times book review of the Da Vinci Code claimed it was right up there with myths about Roswell and Loch Ness. Roswell quickly attained worldwide fame some 40 years after the 1947 "Incident" when a number of people began remembering their experiences for "researchers" wanting to write books about them.

Doc Noss' gold find at Victorio Peak, on the White Sands Missile Range, northeast of Hatch, appeared to be on its way to worldwide fame but books have not been forthcoming, at least yet, on the latest chapters involving purported government looting of the treasure and the subsequent unwillingness of the missile range to allow the Noss heirs back to the restricted area.

Otherwise, in Billy the Kid land, the judge in the Silver City request to exhume Catherine Antrim, Billy's mother, has postponed that hearing, so Billy's lawyers have moved on to Fort Sumner and are again channeling Billy. They can do this because they are from Santa Fe. A city council candidate a few years ago channeled deceased artist Tommy Macaione, who during his lifetime had run for mayor, governor and president.

In Fort Sumner, Billy testified that he wanted to be dug up. His lawyers admitted in their motion for Billy to be heard that "This is a unique moment in jurisprudence where law, history, legend, myth and modern criminology come simultaneously to the forefront in a single proceeding."

Many are now starting to ask why Governor Bill Richardson has involved himself with this case, which was begun by the sheriffs of Lincoln and De Baca counties.

In a reply to the attorneys, whom the governor appointed for Billy, lawyers for Silver City stated, "The primary question remains: Why has Governor Bill Richardson personally involved himself in the Billy the Kid case, which is a travesty of the law, of science and of history?"

The brief concludes: "The attempt by the governor to use executive powers to intervene in a district court to control the outcome of a legal case is of a magnitude serious enough to initiate questions of whether the governor should be subject to recall."

10

GOVERNOR AND SHERIFFS JOIN UP

(Published April 14, 2004)

Governor Bill Richardson should disassociate himself from the effort to dig up Billy's bones. A project that this column supported, when it began last summer, has taken on a touch of the macabre with an almost complete fixation on digging up bodies.

Last June, when Lincoln County Sheriff Tom Sullivan and Deputy Steve Sederwall, who also is the Capitan mayor, announced they were reopening the case of Billy the Kid, this column applauded the effort as a boon to tourism. Soon they had lined up De Baca County Sheriff Gary Graves and all came to Santa Fe to see Governor Richardson.

The governor, actually, was already on board, so they had a big media event in the cabinet room. The sheriffs were dressed in their best cowboy sheriff attire. Life-size pictures of Billy and former Lincoln County Sheriff Pat Garrett adorned the room. Those pictures now hang on the walls of the State Police security office just inside the doors to the governor's inner sanctum of offices.

The sheriffs allowed as how there still were some loose ends to tie up in a 122-year-old criminal investigation. Pat

Garrett hadn't done much of an investigation of Billy shooting his two deputies, because Billy already was sentenced to hang for murdering former Sheriff Brady.

And then, of course, there was that little matter of guys in Texas and Arizona claiming they were Billy and had escaped when Garrett shot someone else and said it was Billy. For his part, the governor said he needed to know if he should fulfill then-Governor Lew Wallace's promise of a pardon for Billy.

They all denied the investigation was a cheap publicity stunt to promote tourism but there seemed to be a great amount of winking going on. And no one interested in promoting tourism appeared to have any complaints about the plan.

Digging up bodies was mentioned, but so was digging bullets out of the Lincoln County Courthouse walls and the centerpiece of the effort, from listening to the governor, was to be a series of hearings to be held in Silver City, Las Cruces, Lincoln and Fort Sumner. The governor said he would appoint a prosecutor and defense counsel to present evidence from Billy's various encounters with the law. They would be great media events and would draw attention to various areas of the state.

But the only appointments Governor Richardson has made so far are two defense counsels to represent Billy in actual courts of law. And here the situation becomes absurd. Only the court can appoint an attorney, but not for someone who already is dead. The dead have no standing in court, but the attorneys are speaking for them. Preposterous.

This now has gone from a tongue-in-cheek romp through New Mexico history to a dead serious matter. These sheriffs really want those bones and at this point, the governor is right in there with them.

And what happens if this ghoulish exercise results in finding matching DNA in the graves of Billy and his mother? We will know what history already has told us. There will be some publicity at the time. Tourists will still come look at the graves, as they did before.

And what happens if a DNA match isn't found? Since media prefer the negative, we'll get substantial coverage and who will want to come look at the graves anymore?

The odds of the latter are extremely high. The state Office of the Medical Investigator says the probability of finding useful DNA is so unlikely after 120 years that the exhumation request should not be granted. In addition, the OMI points out, the cemeteries where Billy and his mother were buried both were ravaged by floods that carried away headstones and some bodies. And subsequently, Catherine Antrim's gravesite was moved.

The governor and sheriffs should realize that overriding the OMI, on which all New Mexico law enforcement depends, is extremely ill-advised and precedent setting. And by the way, the OMI's position turns out to be very different from what the sheriffs' attorney Sherry Tippett originally told us.

So why are the governor and sheriffs still so intent on digging up bodies, even if it is likely to hurt tourism? I can't imagine, but we'll look into it.

And while we're looking, we'll also check out the assurances from the sheriffs that no taxpayer money is being spent on this adventure.

11

WHY IS BILLY SO FAMOUS?

(Published April 23, 2004)

The Case of Billy's Bones has not made big news in New Mexico thus far, but among many Billy the Kid historians and aficionados around the world, it is an unfathomable defiling of sacred ground. And there is very big news still to be uncovered.

To historians, the effort to dig up the bones of Billy and his mother is an insult to history. Billy's life and death have been carefully researched over the years. To them, there is no doubt that Sheriff Pat Garrett shot Billy at Pete Maxwell's house.

Billy's body was laid out all night in Fort Sumner, while women from the community conducted a vigil for someone they had come to admire. There was no doubt in any of their minds that it was Billy lying on the carpenter's table. The coroner's jury arrived the following morning and reached the same conclusion.

Billy was subsequently buried beside his pals Tom O'Folliard and Charlie Bowdre and has remained there ever since. As Frederick W. Nolan, the world's preeminent Lincoln County War historian puts it, the legend of Billy rests on a "delicate balance." If that balance is tilted by doubt about whether he was killed that night and whether he was buried where his gravesite stands, then the legend decays.

And that is exactly what is at risk if a DNA match between Billy and his mother cannot be established after all these years even if the correct bones are found. Then the claims of other pretenders, such as Brushy Bill, of Hico, Texas, make it plausible that Billy escaped and lived an uneventful life elsewhere.

How did this homeless, drifting, juvenile delinquent turned outlaw, who died at 21, end up in Webster's International Dictionary alongside Alexander the Great, Napoleon and George Washington? Why does he have one of the highest name recognitions throughout the world of any American historical figure? Why is his grave site one of the few in America identified on state maps and some national ones?

Gale Cooper, a Harvard-educated psychiatrist and amateur historian, has some answers. She has just completed what she says is the most extensively researched historical novel on Billy the Kid and the Lincoln County War ever written.

Dr. Cooper says the Billy the Kid legend is the epitome of the West. Like all great legends, it resonates with all generations and cultures and retranslates depending on who you are. It can be the epic hero journey of the boy Billy, dying as a martyred freedom fighter, a rebel with a cause. Or it can be a terrifying morality tale of an outlaw whose murderous rampage was ended by the righteous power of a lawman.

Fort Sumner residents report that people come to their village from all parts of the world to visit his grave. Those from countries who have known oppression are especially attracted to the grave site of someone who was a freedom fighter in the Old West of America. Some will even wear cowboy clothes they've obviously just purchased, so they can share more deeply in the emotion of the moment.

They also report a following that reveres Billy's grave. Some visit his grave at night to pay their regards, lighting candles and leaving gifts, flowers, love notes, bullets and unopened cans of beer. Often, on July 14, the anniversary of Billy's 1881 death, a vigil is held, remembering a similar vigil by many of the ladies of the community 122 years ago.

Scholars say Jesse James and Wyatt Earp, who both inspire big followings, don't produce the passion among their followers that the legend of Billy does. Somehow it resonates with stronger vibrations to create a subculture of Billy worshipers worldwide.

The test of great epics is their ability to transcend time. It is quite clear that the passage of 122 years since his death has only increased the fame and fascination of Billy the Kid.

Let's not do anything to destroy that.

12

MY IDEAS FOR PROMOTING BILLY

(Published May 2, 2004)

Here's my contribution to a positive resolution of the current Billy the Kid controversy.

This column has said there are better ways than digging up bodies to prove whether Pat Garrett shot Billy or let him get away. There also are better ways to prove whether any of Billy's pretenders were the real thing. And there are better ways to improve sagging tourism in Billy the Kid Country.

The three sheriffs now are saying what they really want is to determine what happened in the Lincoln County Courthouse the day Billy escaped and left two deputies dead. Did he have an accomplice who left him a gun in the outhouse, with which to shoot the first deputy?

I'll admit to not having a ready answer for that. Billy already had been sentenced to death for killing Sheriff Brady so there wasn't much investigation done at the time. If the sheriffs would confine their investigation to that matter, and forget about digging up graves, everyone might be happy and the sheriffs might contribute something to the Billy legend.

Here's my proposal for other activities:

1. Compare Billy's handwriting and photograph with those of his pretenders. Tim Evans, who produced "Billy the Kid Unmasked" for the Discovery Channel recently, has had a photographic analysis done already. It is possible he would get a handwriting analysis done too, since he has told me he would like to do a second program.

2. Hold the four hearings around Billy the Kid Country that Governor Richardson enthused about when he announced his support for the sheriff's project. Several Billy the Kid scholars have told me they are willing to help.

The scholars, the sheriffs and others, as appropriate, could serve as expert witnesses. In order to make the hearings interesting to a public conditioned to fast-moving TV specials, maybe the scripts could be written using Governor Richardson's contacts in the film industry, assisted by students in the screen writing classes that will be funded by the $10 million appropriation requested by the governor and approved by the 2004 Legislature for beefing up the New Mexico film industry's infrastructure.

The governor also could use his contacts to promote the hearings as media events. Billy the Kid is better known around the world than O.J. Simpson was before his trial. Such extravaganzas aren't unknown to New Mexico. The trial of the accused killers of Albert Jennings Fountain, who defended Billy at his murder trial, drew hordes of reporters from all over the planet–and that was over a century ago, in tiny Hillsboro, NM.

3. Some of that $10 million the Legislature appropriated for New Mexico's film effort could be used as a prize for the best film script on the life and death of Billy. And the state's kitty for producing movies in and about New Mexico would be quite an enticement for getting the movie shot here in the actual locations.

4. The History Channel and the Discovery Channel already have featured Billy's legend this year. With increasing interest in the current Billy controversy, network television may be ready for it.

5. Governor Richardson could find money for a major writing competition with prizes for the best new fiction and non-fiction books on Billy. The non-fiction category would be especially good for encouraging new research into the legend.

6. The state Tourism Department could develop a Billy the Kid Circle Tour of the state, featuring not only the communities that already promote their relation to Billy, but some like Silver City, Roswell, Las Vegas and Santa Fe that haven't featured him in the past.

7. And the capstone of it all would be a grand 125th Anniversary Commemoration of Billy's final months of life, featuring those communities in which the action was taking place at the time. July 2006 is the anniversary of Billy's death. Events could start many months earlier. And the grand finale would include awarding of the prizes for best research, best novel and best movie.

There's my ideas. I'd love to hear yours.

13

I BEGIN DIGGING

(Published May 28, 2004)

The three sheriffs are still intent on digging up Billy the Kid and his mother despite the fact that it makes no sense. They continue their criminal investigation to determine whether then-sheriff Pat Garrett shot Billy or someone else.

More than ample historical evidence exists, including the report of a coroner's jury, to prove that Garrett shot the Kid. Photographic evidence has determined that Billy's two main pretenders didn't look anything like him. Handwriting analysis very likely would demonstrate the same.

But the sheriffs want to use the magic of DNA to prove their case despite the fact that DNA testing loses its magic after 120 years, according to the state Office of the Medical Investigator. Further complicating the matter is the lack of certainty about exactly where the bodies are buried and the fact that local authorities do not want them disturbed.

The sheriffs also indicated that they felt their investigation would promote tourism in their counties. There was talk of hearings to be conducted throughout Billy the Kid country that would cast further light on the legend and attract national and international attention.

This column supported that notion for several months until it became evident that digging up bodies was the all-consuming intent of the venture. Instead of informal hearings to offer historical evidence, the sheriffs went to court in Silver City and Fort Sumner to force unwilling communities to let them dig.

Considering the overwhelming evidence against a DNA match, the possibility of solving a crime is very low and the likelihood that it will destroy a legend for the communities is high. State Tourism Department statistics show that although tourism in Southern New Mexico was up last year, tourism in Billy the Kid country was down.

In a column last month, we promised to look into why the sheriffs are so intent on digging and to check out their assurances that no taxpayer money is being spent on this adventure. Here's what we've found so far.

On May 13, I filed requests for financial and other information concerning the official activities of Lincoln County Sheriff Tom Sullivan; Capitan Mayor Steve Sederwall, who represents himself as a deputy sheriff of Lincoln County; and DeBaca County Sheriff Gary Graves, in relation to the Billy the Kid case.

As of May 24, I have received no response from Mr. Sederwall, who is also running for county commissioner on June 1. And the responses I received with regard to Sullivan and Graves were inadequate and disturbing.

Attorney General Patricia Madrid states that "the public's access to government actions is a crucial aspect of a functioning democracy." The law requires public access to virtually all public records. Anytime any public entity enters into any formal or informal agreement, it takes on a responsibility to the public for a financial accounting of its acts and financial accounts.

These records must stand the light of day. This includes the responsibility to inform the public of any funding, public or private, in order to protect each taxpayer's right to judge potential conflicts of interest or other areas of concern.

New Mexico law imposes a record-keeping responsibility for any public entity with regard to payroll, vouchers, expenditures, use of vehicles or services, and income so that undue influence or misuse of public or private funds in public endeavors can be judged. Obtaining any of these records for review and audit is the right of any citizen.

A major concern with this case is that it has been made a law enforcement matter in both Lincoln and DeBaca counties, since Sullivan, Sederwall and Graves are conducting it as a criminal investigation of a 122-year-old murder. According to Lincoln County Commissioner Leo Martinez, families of much more recent murder victims feel strongly that the sheriffs should be spending their time on those cases.

I want to be fair, but I'm concerned about the lack of response by Sederwall and the nature of the responses from Sullivan and Graves. I will give them another opportunity to make their records available to the public and hope they will do a better job of clarifying their involvement in this case.

14

SHERIFFS CAN'T EXPLAIN

(Published June 9, 2004)

The criminal investigation of the three sheriffs who want to dig up Billy the Kid and his mom has never made sense on any level.

Sometimes the sheriffs have contended they are trying to determine whether Sheriff Pat Garrett killed Billy or if he conspired with Billy to kill someone else so the Kid could make a getaway. If that is the case, the jurisdiction is Fort Sumner, in DeBaca County, and Garrett is the accused criminal.

On other occasions the sheriffs have said they want to get to the bottom of what happened in Lincoln at the County Courthouse the day Billy escaped and two deputies were killed. There seems little doubt that Billy was the culprit. The only question may be whether someone helped him get a gun to kill the first deputy. If so, we have a conspiracy charge in Lincoln County, with their claim that Garrett and Billy were buddies- such good buddies that Garrett sneaked him a pistol to kill his own deputy.

Alternatively, the sheriffs have suggested they want to prove that Garrett got his man and that the various pretenders are frauds. Garrett is the patron saint of the Lincoln County Sheriff's Department. His likeness appears on the sheriffs' shoulder patches. Fraud is a crime, so all Billy's pretenders are evidently the suspects.

Everyone we have talked about, thus far, has been dead for anywhere from a half century to almost 125 years. That really doesn't make them an imminent danger to any of us, does it? If Billy somehow escaped Garrett's ambush and still is on the loose today, we shouldn't be too worried about a 145-year old Kid or his long-deceased co-conspirators.

So what the sheriffs are trying to do here is prosecute some dead guys, which is a legal impossibility. Somehow the governor got sucked into this fantasy and has appointed a lawyer to represent Billy. That also can't be done. Only the court can appoint lawyers for defendants–and they have to be alive.

But wait a minute, you say? This is just some good, clean fun to promote tourism in an area of the state that really needs it. Who can disagree with that? Certainly not I, if I felt that were true. But the evidence keeps leading in a different direction.

A great amount of money has been spent on this case already. In the long Probable Cause Statement filed by the Lincoln County Sheriff's Department, a litany of investigative activities on the part of public officials is described. Someone also had to do a significant amount of historical research.

The governor says the lawyer he hired for Billy is doing the work for free, but there are other lawyers also working this case and free legal work involves only a lawyer's time. Someone has to pay the expenses for such costs as telephone, travel, copying and expert witnesses.

Either we taxpayers are paying for this or a very generous individual is bankrolling it for some unimaginable reason. That is what my investigation has been about.

From the skimpy information I have been provided, so far, in my search for public records pertaining to the case, I have been told either that "no public records are responsive" to my requests or that "private funds were expended." I also have been told that this is "an ongoing criminal investigation" so the records I have requested are not subject to disclosure.

That leaves some mighty big questions unanswered. Chief among them is how can public funds and time not be used in a real criminal investigation? And next, who is the sugar daddy giving money to this criminal investigation by public officials? It is our legal right to know who it is so we can make judgments about conflicts of interest.

C,mon now, guys. What do you take us for? We all know this isn't a real case. Why don't you want the financing or expenditures in this case exposed to the light of day? What are you really up to? And who is this case really meant to benefit?

15

YOUR IDEAS FOR PROMOTING BILLY

(Published June 14, 2004)

The suggestions are coming in for alternative ways to promote the Billy the Kid legend in New Mexico.

Dave Clary of Roswell suggests that instead of my idea for scripted hearings, why not conduct moot trials as they do in law schools. Billy could be tried in Lincoln for the murders of Bell and Olinger. Deputy Sheriff Steve Sederwall could be called to testify as to what he has learned from his investigations at the Lincoln County Courthouse.

Some of New Mexico's more colorful prosecutors and defense attorneys could be asked to fill those roles. A state Supreme Court justice could act as judge.

Clary also suggests a special commission, similar to the 9/11 Commission, be appointed by Governor Richardson to advise him on whether he should grant Billy a pardon.

It could look into Governor Lew Wallace's promise of a pardon in exchange for Billy's testimony in another case, whether Billy met those conditions, the circumstances surrounding Wallace's failure to grant a pardon, and maybe even the circumstances surrounding the conduct of Billy's trial that resulted in the only murder conviction in the Lincoln County War.

Trish Saunders of Seattle suggests the commission could conduct an official inquiry into the causes of the Lincoln County War. She also suggests that Billy not be the only one on trial. Bring the other side to justice too.

Clary thinks a novel or movie script would only reflect our own times rather than Billy's time. He suggests an annual student essay contest on New Mexico history, with the first year's topic being Billy the Kid. The governor could present savings bonds or other awards.

But some disagree with Clary, claiming there is a magnificent love story waiting to be written about Billy, complete with names so descriptive of their characters that Dickens couldn't do better.

The Village of Lincoln conducts an annual summer pageant, called The Last Escape of Billy the Kid. That should not be overlooked in planning a statewide commemoration of the 125th anniversary of Billy the Kid's death in 2006. Rose Barton writes that Old Fort Days in Fort Sumner in June shouldn't be overlooked either.

Silver City also is gaining an interest in telling people what happened back in the days when Billy was growing up there. The town now has a Billy the Kid Museum, a marker on his mother's grave and a Billy event has been added to the June Wild, Wild West Pro Rodeo Week.

Sherry Tippett called to say the Mimbres Regional Arts Council is having a fundraiser on June 19 called the Millie and Billy Ball, honoring the town's most colorful madam and outlaw. It will feature a $10,000 drawing.

By the way, the big Peppin Fire, near Capitan, is named for Peppin Canyon where it started. The canyon was named for

George "Dad" Peppin, who was sheriff of Lincoln County in 1878. He led the posse that had Billy and friends trapped in the McSween House, which the posse eventually set on fire. Several of Billy's group were killed or captured, but Billy made one of his famous getaways.

Peppin was serving out the term of Sheriff Brady, whom Billy was convicted of killing. Apparently the canyon was named for him because he owned the property. It's not likely to bear his name because of his prowess as a lawman.

The Peppin Fire also has burned an area associated with another Lincoln County celebrity. The blaze charred the home turf of Smokey Bear, where he was found clinging to a tree 54 years ago.

My thanks to those who contacted me to add their ideas to mine about how to promote the Billy legend. Maybe as a result, more people will become aware of what historians have to tell us about what really happened in the days of the Lincoln County War.

16

FINDING SOME TRUTHS

(Published July 2, 2004)

New evidence arrives almost daily proving that the quest to dig up Billy and his mom is the most bizarre case in the history of jurisprudence.

It is amazing that it still is in the courts, but the Village of Fort Sumner has filed a motion to dismiss the case and sets out the issues in a manner that can't be avoided.

The situation would actually be comical if it didn't adversely affect two communities so strongly. Silver City and Fort Sumner face a loss of their part of the Billy the Kid legend if DNA analysis is unable to show a match between bones dug up in the two communities.

The state Office of the Medical Investigator says that is likely because of the lack of certainty about the exact location of the bodies and the low quality of DNA in corpses over 120 years old. Sentiment also runs high in both communities about the sanctity of their cemeteries and the impropriety of digging up bodies.

The scenario is playing out like an Old West melodrama with plenty of victims and villains (some of them dressed in 1880s sheriffs' outfits). Currently, however, the plot outline is too garbled for a good melodrama. It is playing out more like the Keystone Cops at this point.

The three sheriffs involved in the case are running around, simultaneously conducting a criminal investigation of whom Pat Garrett shot and whether Billy had help escaping the Lincoln County Courthouse, while also trying to prove that Billy is buried in Fort Sumner and that his pretenders are fakes.

Add to that their efforts to help the governor decide whether to pardon Billy and also to help the governor promote tourism. Oh yes, and they're collecting antique furniture and shooting it.

What do all these cross-purposes have to do with each other? I promised to seek that out, but I can't tell you yet. I'm getting closer to discovering the thread that binds all this together, but still haven't found the universal truth.

And speaking of truth, that has become the mantra of the two spokesmen for the grave digging, Governor Bill Richardson and Capitan Mayor Steve Sederwall, who also is a sometimes deputy sheriff. I've discovered, however, that he is only a reserve deputy, a volunteer, so to speak.

Like Fox Mulder in X-Files, Richardson and Sederwall know "the truth is out there" but evil forces prevent it from being known. In this case, it is the towns of Silver City and Fort Sumner, and although they may not be evil, they are anti-scientific and anti-historical in their determination to not let scientific grave robbers into their cemeteries.

But maybe the truth isn't "out there." Maybe it is here among us. The petition filed by Fort Sumner to dismiss the court action seeking to exhume Billy lists many truths. Among them are:

- The New Mexico Supreme Court, in a previous decision, has expressed a strong predisposition against disinterment.
- The petitioners have no legal relationship to Billy.
- A dead person can't seek relief.
- A governor can't appoint a lawyer, even for someone who isn't dead.
- A coroner's jury already ruled in 1881 on who shot Billy.
- Reopening the case would be double jeopardy.
- The statute of limitations for any criminal investigation expired long ago.
- The job of the sheriffs is to protect the public. There is no criminal on the loose.

Actually the truth may be much nearer than we think. Billy's gubernatorially-appointed attorney has been speaking for him, making claims that Billy wants to be dug up and wants his mother dug up.

Since Billy is speaking from the grave, and since his attorney is communicating with him, the attorney has to know where Billy is buried. All he has to do is tell us and it's all over.

Case closed.

17

A SHELL GAME

(Published August 9, 2004)

The three sheriffs trying to dig up Billy the Kid and his mother are a slippery bunch of varmints. Their responses to my information requests have been full of contradictions and pieces that don't fit together.

The sheriffs claim they are conducting an official criminal investigation, so they can't tell me anything about what they are doing or how much time and money they are spending on the investigation.

That is important information to me because I contend that they are wasting a great amount of time and taxpayer money going after possible criminals who committed their acts over a century ago. And all they are accomplishing is the likely destruction of a legend that no longer will be able to boost tourism in Silver City and Fort Sumner.

But at other times, the sheriffs tell me the total investigation is funded with private money and they don't have to tell me about that either. It seems highly unlikely that private money is paying their salaries and funding the operation of their offices while they spend time on their investigation, but it may be paying many other expenses.

So what are we to make of a privately-funded criminal investigation? Is that good public policy? It does save taxpayer money. But think about it. What happens if rich folks can fund criminal investigations? They can take over New Mexico law enforcement. They can go after whomever they want. It sounds like vigilante justice.

It also sounds a lot like the infamous Santa Fe Ring that controlled sheriffs and district attorneys and judges back in Billy's day. That's what Billy and John Tunstall and Alexander McSween were fighting against.

Is history repeating itself? Well, it's probably not that bad, but someone is putting a large amount of money into financing a criminal investigation. And we have a right by law to know who it is.

Private money entering public coffers to be used for operational purposes must be open to sunshine laws. In this case, it becomes part of an official criminal investigation by public officials, thereby "changing color" and becoming subject to public scrutiny.

But the current situation is totally different. The sheriffs are shielding the identity of their benefactor and the use of all money received. Depending on their audience, they are shielding that information either as part of a criminal investigation or as the act of private citizens doing some privately-funded research on their own.

In fact, sometimes, they're just three good old boys out having fun, proclaiming that it will be good for tourism and maybe there might even be a book or movie deal in it.

The public has a right to know what is happening. Where is the money coming from and for what hidden purpose? This intrigue extends all the way up to the governor and apparently there is more than one anonymous benefactor. The public has a right know what, if anything, these benefactors are receiving in return.

At this point, the sheriffs are playing a shell game with us. They said they are really conducting an "ongoing criminal investigation." That should mean taxpayer expenses. But Sullivan and Graves claim "private" benefactors and Sederwall surprisingly told the Attorney General that he was using his "own private funds."

The sheriffs claim their "criminal investigation" shields them from releasing information. That would be information about "criminals," but not information about where the money is coming from.

The fact is that the sheriffs can't shield themselves from scrutiny by claiming that any of their acts are private since they are all public officials conducting a very public case.

And what about Deputy Sederwall, who seems to be doing most of the leg work in this investigation. He presents himself as a deputy, authorized to conduct a criminal investigation and dig up bodies, but when I inquired as to the conditions of his deputizing, I was told he is only a "reserve" deputy, a title that doesn't even appear in state statutes.

We'll keep after this until all the pieces fit together.

Billy the Kid historian Frederick Nolan of Chalfont St. Giles, England

18

FREDERICK NOLAN WEIGHS IN

(Published August 20, 2004)

On New Year's eve last year, Sheriff Tom Sullivan and Steve Sederwall, calling himself a Deputy Sheriff, filed the Billy the Kid case murder investigation Probable Cause Statement in state District Court in Silver City. It is the parent document used to try to dig up Billy and his mother to solve a supposed murder by Pat Garrett of an unknown cowboy, not Billy.

I'm trying to solve what those sheriffs are doing with their law enforcement time and budget, so I decided to look at it myself.

A probable cause statement gives legal reasons for arrest. Well, Garrett, the suspect, has been dead for 96 years. So if we leave out that a case doesn't exist, we are left with 13 questionable pages that have pieces of history, more footnotes than a farm dog has fleas, and an affidavit. It left me with questions, so I went to the man recognized as the world's pre-eminent Billy the Kid historian, Frederick Nolan of Chalfont St. Giles, England.

Nolan's response was straightforward. The statement made no sense. He called it "a shameful and semi-literate criminal investigation that indeed is criminal but not an investigation," and "a charade foisted on the American people."

The sheriffs' statement begins by saying that "investigators" of the Lincoln County War learned that "nothing was as it seemed." Sounds intriguing, except that Nolan would like to know the qualifications of these anonymous "investigators", since no credible expert in the highly researched field ever said that nothing was as it seemed. Next the document claims "newly discovered evidence." Sounds good again, but there's none to be found.

What follows should be a "probable cause," meaning evidence that Garrett killed another kid. But Nolan finds only a grab bag of facts which range from the murder of John Tunstall in 1878 to the shooting of Deputy Bell in 1881, which are "totally irrelevant to the question of whether Garrett shot Billy the Kid." Rather pathetically, there isn't even an attempt to answer the most obvious question of Garrett's motive. He certainly had one to shoot the real Kid. He was sheriff and deputy U.S. marshal and Billy was arguably the most notorious outlaw/murderer in the country.

Nolan notes that the "investigators" present only one fact: "On March 23, Governor Wallace met with William Bonney (Kid) in Lincoln." But Nolan discloses that it was March 17th. That leaves "considerable doubt about their ability to handle facts." To say nothing of the fact that Wallace's meeting (in 1879) is irrelevant to the case at hand.

Nolan noted that the sheriffs "make much of the involvement of David S. Turk of the U.S. Marshal's Service." A search by Nolan produced only two books by Turk, both by an obscure press and neither having to do with Billy the Kid. Nolan calls Turk's involvement "window dressing."

And the footnoted quotes either don't prove what they claim or are misleadingly out of context. Paco Anaya is quoted from his book to prove the body was not Billy's. Only problem is that he knew Billy well and the name of his book is *I Buried Billy*.

The Affidavit that ends the document is by a man who swore that in 1940 when he was nine, Garrett's widow told him Garrett didn't shoot the Kid. Unfortunately she died in 1936. Nolan also was incensed by a quote from historian Robert Utley's book which just says that Garrett's book on the Kid had errors. Not only is that irrelevant to the case, but citing Utley out of context is nothing more than shameless name dropping, he says.

Nolan feels that saying Garrett did not shoot the Kid is so bizarre that it belongs in "the birthplace of the flying saucer legend." He contends, "The entire document is either a hoax or a tissue of inventions and half-truths which cast serious doubt upon the motives and integrity of the Lincoln County Sheriff's Department." He concludes, "This is not history. It's just smoke and mirrors."

19

FOOLING ONLY SOME OF THE PEOPLE

(Published September 1, 2004)

It seems about time the three sheriffs, looking for Billy's body, accept the fact that you can fool some of the people some of the time, but not all of the people all of the time.

So far, they have avoided reporting who is paying for their shenanigans with the Billy the Kid case by changing hats. They say it's a real criminal investigation, so its records are shielded. But everyone knows taxpayer money pays for law enforcement. "No," they say, private donors paid. They even imply the case is their history hobby. The catch is that hat changing does not work. It is a public case, they are public officials, and public and private money are subject to audit.

When it comes to the deputizing of Capitan Mayor Steve Sederwall by Lincoln County Sheriff Tom Sullivan, it is just as slippery. Mr. Sederwall calls himself Deputy Sheriff in the criminal investigation filed by the Lincoln County Sheriff's Department in which Pat Garrett is the alleged murderer and an unknown cowboy, not the Kid, is his victim. And on every petition to the District Courts of De Baca and Grant counties to dig up Billy or his mother, Deputy Sederwall is a co-petitioner.

But when I checked on his status, I was told he is a "reserve" deputy and that no paperwork was done. "Reserve" deputy is not in New Mexico statutes; special deputy and regular deputy are. The first is only for serving writs or preserving the peace. The second requires a good deal of written documentation and a sworn oath of office. Obviously none of this has been done.

So it seems Sullivan and Sederwall have tried to pull a fast one. But there's a catch. Sederwall may be a fake deputy, but having represented himself as a public official conducting the Billy the Kid case, he is now subject to public scrutiny as to money spent.

Most recently the three sheriffs have wheeled out forensic expert Dr. Henry Lee, of O.J. Simpson defense notoriety, to find blood on the carpenter's bench on which the dead Billy allegedly lay. Paid for by Kurtis Productions of the History Channel, Dr. Lee, according to newspaper accounts, did field tests and found blood on the bench.

The only problem is the chemical he sprayed, called Luminol, also gives positive reactions to bacteria, metals, and detergents. But he's heading with his "scrapings" to a lab called Orchid Cellmark.

I checked with forensic experts around the country and learned blood has never been proven to exist over about 50 years. Dead Billy bled 123 years ago. And lab tests can falsely indicate blood if iron compounds like rust are present along with DNA, which could come from saliva or a sneeze on the bench a month ago.

Moving on from the smoke screen of a "CSI investigation," if the carpenter's bench is historically real - and the only accepted bench belongs to the Maxwell family - then three generations have preserved it. Can anyone seriously believe that a family would keep that old, dirty thing for three generations because an unknown cowboy and not Billy lay on it?

And if the dead Billy was on it, the sheriffs have disproved their own case. Of course, they want us to believe they can get DNA from it and head back after the bones of Billy and his mother. But the location of their remains cannot be substantiated. There's nowhere to go to match DNA.

What the three sheriffs need is not DNA, but more suckers. One is supposed to be born every minute, so we wish them luck. But right now the Billy the Kid case looks like a criminal case where the victim isn't an unknown cowboy, but the New Mexico taxpayers and anyone hoping that officers of the law work on real crimes committed by real criminals.

20

DR. HENRY LEE EMERGES

(Published September 5, 2004)

Our three Sherlockian sheriffs keep plugging away at the Billy the Kid Case, their "criminal investigation" of whether Garrett killed the Kid, despite the fact that legitimate historians are not buying that any case exists.

Their latest move is adding forensic expert Dr. Henry Lee, who received media attention, though not great credibility, helping defend O.J. Simpson. They brought him here to test their carpenter's bench on which they claim dead Billy lay, a shot up washstand, and floorboards in the old Lincoln County Courthouse. From those few hours of swabbing and scraping, he concluded that the Billy the Kid Case was "legitimate."

How could Dr. Lee make that leap of faith? I decided to get opinions about the case from the country's most prominent forensic experts. Tom Mauriello, author of a textbook on forensic science, director of a crime lab for 27 years, and consultant on a Discovery Channel program on ax-murderer Lizzie Borden said, "Dr. Lee claimed he found blood on the bench, but the Luminol he used also tests positive for bacteria, detergents, and metal."

Lee said he used laser technology to determine the trajectory of the washstand's bullet. But Mauriello says "a trajectory is meaningless if you don't know the locations of Pat,

Billy, or the washstand at the crime scene." And it has nothing to do with whether Pat Garrett killed the Kid anyway.

Dr. Clyde Snow, perhaps the world's most famous forensic anthropologist doing cases both criminal and historical and as varied as remains from Custer's last stand, Tutankhamen, victims of the Oklahoma City bombing, as well as mass graves in atrocities against humanity said, "It is not ethically responsible for a forensic expert to take on a case of historical nature which involves exhumation, unless professional historians feel that it merits scientific inquiry.
I would not participate in the Billy the Kid case for that reason," Snow said. He also added, "Science can never prove that flying saucers do not exist." I took that as a polite way of saying that the case belongs in science fiction, not science.

Dr. Edward Blake, DNA forensic expert at Forensic Sciences Associates in California, added that he does not know of any blood sample significantly greater than 50 years old that is small and has been successfully typed using DNA technology. Billy's blood would be 123 years old.

Brian Wraxall, a 40-year forensic expert in DNA, working at Serological Research Institute in California and trained in Scotland Yard, pointed out more problems for Dr. Lee. All he can hope for in his next step of taking his sample to Orchid Cellmark lab is finding human DNA. But that would not prove blood or its age.

The DNA could be from a sneeze last week. And "DNA would accumulate from everyone who contacted that bench over the years. And once DNA mixes, it cannot be separated." He also said the obvious: "If Billy bled on it, someone that day would have washed it off." Billy was not a saint from whom you would save relics.

In fact Dr. Blake felt that since the bench is not 100 percent provable as authentic, there is not even a starting point for a chain of evidence. He said, "The kindest thing I can say about the three sheriffs is that they are pulling a hoax in order to get their names in the paper."

And in our own New Mexico Office of the Medical Investigator, Director Dr. Ross Zumwalt and forensic anthropologist Dr. Debra Komar already have refused exhumation in the case since the location of the bodies is uncertain. So there is no DNA for comparison.

Wraxall said the case reminded him of "a police line up with no reference picture of the criminal."

So we have Dr. Lee's sample that can never be proven to be old or blood or from just one person that he wants to match with remains with uncertain identities to figure out if Pat killed Billy.

It doesn't look good.

21

THE LINCOLN COUNTY HOAX

(Published September 8, 2004)

The three sheriffs, tirelessly pushing the Billy the Kid case for a year, may have accomplished their goal, though not exactly as they intended.

Lacking historical expertise or the advice of an expert historian, they have nevertheless tried to change the history of Pat Garrett and Billy the Kid. Since few doubted the story of Pat killing the Kid, it occurred to me that the sheriffs wanted to make a contribution to New Mexico history. And I think they did.

There hasn't been a world-class historical hoax since the early 1900's when a man named Charles Dawson claimed to have found the "missing link" in a gravel pit in England. He called his pieces of braincase and chunk of jawbone Piltdown Man. It took almost 50 years for someone to realize it was an orangutan's jaw with filed down teeth and 600 year old skull pieces. Why did Dawson do it? Well, he gave Piltdown Man his name: "dawsoni." And maybe it was his version of "punked" humor.

The Piltdown Hoax probably has not had competition because it takes almost as much work to pull off a great historical hoax as to conduct actual research. I'm not counting the Loch Ness monster. Monsters are easy. You just say you saw one and take a blurry photograph.

Webster's Dictionary says to hoax is "to trick into accepting as genuine something false and often preposterous." That brings up the missing link in a hoax: people who believe preposterous things. Seems we hit the magic moment. The sheriffs may have created history's Frankenstein's monster.

The famous Billy the Kid historian Frederick Nolan called the sheriffs' criminal case Probable Cause statement a hoax because it looks for all the world like a heavily researched document chock full of footnotes. Except not a single reference has to do with whether Garrett killed Billy. Since many of the sources are rare or on microfilm it is not too far fetched to think that they never dreamed that anyone would check it out. But they were wrong.

The case is also set up as a murder investigation with "evidence." Part of that evidence is the alleged carpenter's bench on which dead Billy lay. Dr Henry Lee, a forensic expert, famous for seeking limelight and paid by the History Channel, was brought in to find blood on it. And by golly within hours, he did.

Lee is proceeding to test it for DNA. The problem is that forensic experts around the country said that blood has never been proven to exist much over 50 years. But it was announced in a newspaper that Attorney Bill Robins would again offer his services, this time to take that "DNA" back to Silver City in hopes of getting at Billy's mother's bones.

Since the case is a real criminal investigation, courts have to be tricked also. The hardest trick is obviously calling it a criminal investigation when Garrett, the criminal, has been dead for 96 years. And the case was closed in 1881. It also was discovered that Mayor of Capitan Steve Sederwall, who participated in the case as a deputy sheriff, wasn't one at all.

Motivation is a fascinating part of hoaxing. Fame is tempting. There has been talk of book and film deals. But since these public officials used their time and workplaces for the case, I would throw in the possibility of personal gain at taxpayer expense.

But thanks to the three sheriffs, now New Mexico may not only be home to the Legend of Billy the Kid, but also may be the birthplace of the Lincoln County Hoax: the greatest of them all!

22

BILLY'S BIG DAY

(Published September 12, 2004)

If you are Billy the Kid you can have big days when you're alive and when you're dead. That's one advantage of being famous. And coming up on September 27th is one of the biggest days in Billy's history.

Of course, his hanging trial in Mesilla on April 9, 1881, his great escape from the old Lincoln County Courthouse on April 28 of that same year, and his shooting death by Pat Garrett a few months later on July 14 rank up at the top. But September 27 will be the day when the De Baca County District Court in Fort Sumner will decide if his bones will be allowed to lie at rest, and if what will be buried is the three sheriffs' criminal case. That is why I have Billy on the brain this month.

Over the past year we have seen the mayors and county commissioners of Silver City and Fort Sumner united in opposition to the attempts to get at the bones of Billy and his mother in their respective cemeteries. We have had the Office of the Medical Investigator refuse exhumation permits. We have heard Frederick Nolan, the preeminent historian of the subject, and Dr. Edward Blake, arguably the country's most prominent forensic expert in DNA analysis, calling it a hoax. But we have not seen any sign of its perpetrators backing down.

Dr. Gale Cooper, a Harvard trained M.D. psychiatrist and an amateur historian, whom I had quoted before on the reason the Billy the Kid Legend has such a powerful hold on its fans, said, "I have followed the case closely. And it appears to me that these citizens and experts are not only responding to the specifics of the case, but are reacting to the brazen use of police and executive power to manufacture misinformation for personal gain. There seems to be an attempt to profit from the reflected glory of a famous and cherished piece of history of the American West. What the promulgators may not have realized is that moral outrage is a more powerful motivator than greed in making people take a stand."

Historians and scientists already have taken their stand on the Lincoln County Hoax. Now it will have its day in court. The tone of the three sheriffs' case was already set in March when the Texas lawyer, Bill Robins, brought in by Governor Richardson, using only dead Billy as a client, petitioned the court to remove respected Judge Ricky Purcell. And he was removed.

Attorney Adam Baker of Kennedy & Han and Attorney Herb Marsh will be arguing for dismissal of the case. And Fort Sumner Mayor Raymond Lopez will be standing for his village. They will be arguing that the case be thrown out for many reasons. It is not a criminal investigation since there is no criminal (Pat Garrett is dead) and no investigation.

The case was closed in 1881, so to reopen it is double jeopardy. Since it is not real, the three sheriffs have no right to be in court as officers of the law. And they have no other reason.

The case has no historical merit because evidence supports beyond a reasonable doubt that Garrett killed the Kid. And the case can never establish the contrary, since the precise location of the remains of Billy and his mother are uncertain, so DNA is useless for comparison. Lastly their client dead Billy does not exist.

The Lincoln County Hoax is about to have its day in court on September 27, 2004. All except for the three sheriffs, their legal henchmen, and those hoping to profit from their caper, hope it will be its last.

So if you want to be a part of New Mexico history in the making, the place to be is Fort Sumner on September 27th. I'll be there myself.

23

THE MYSTERIOUS MR. ROBINS

(Published September 15, 2004)

The mysterious attorney Bill Robins, appointed by Governor Bill Richardson last November to represent the dead Billy, arrived like an action hero just in the nick of time, as the effort to exhume Billy's mother was faltering in the Silver City District Court.

And on top of those heroics, Robins offered his work pro bono. Also, there have been rumors he is helping to pay the costs. In my mind, an attorney who not only works for free, but also foots the bills, automatically qualifies as a super hero.

Robins wouldn't have been so mysterious had he just stuck with representing dead Billy. Sure, his legal ploy of having the deceased request his own and his mother's exhumation left me a little queasy. But I would have merely criticized him for a warped sense of humor.

Unfortunately, he also became one of the attorneys joining the three sheriffs in their petition to dig up Billy's mother. And he represented the sheriffs in their petition to dig Billy up. Now it is reported that he plans to represent the sheriffs if they go back to Silver City with their supposed DNA scraped off a supposed carpenter's bench on which the dead Billy lay.

The Web page for Heard, Robins, Lubel, Cloud, and Greenwood LLP," the name of the Houston, Texas law firm with which Robins is associated, has branches in Santa Fe and Hobbs. In business since 1998, these enterprising men whose practice is civil litigation in personal injury, product liability, medical malpractice, class action cases, and representation of Fortune 500 companies, brought in "an excess of 50 million dollars" for their clients in 2001.

An Internet source indicates the firm contributed $25,000 to Governor Richardson's political committee and Robins topped it off with $48,100 more. Reports indicate the firm also contributed generously to other statewide candidates.

Robin's law firm has the slogan "dedicated to their clients needs." It appears as though it is. But who was Robins' client in the Billy the Kid case? Richardson hired him. Since he represents New Mexico, it means the state did too. But Robins says in his court documents that he represents dead Billy.

Leaving the spirit world out of this, the dead do not exist in a court of law. That leaves only the governor and the state as clients, plus the three sheriffs. That means attorney Robins is participating in a New Mexico criminal investigation into murder as an act of charity for the governor, the state, and the police.

But it gets more sticky. An attorney can be appointed only by a judge and for someone indigent. The governor is not a judge. Billy is not indigent; he's dead. And the sheriffs and Lincoln County, which they brought in, aren't indigent either. So can someone solve the mystery of why Attorney Robins came in the first place, and how did he get into our courts?

Try a different angle. If Robins can speak FOR the dead Billy, he must be able to speak TO him. Then why didn't Billy hire him? In fact, by hiring Robins, Richardson proved that he is the client.

Don't get me wrong. I'm in favor of pals. After all, New Mexico has immortalized the concept on the Billy the Kid tombstone, which has "pals" carved in granite. So maybe Attorney Robins is best pals with our governor.

Then they can explain to all of us lacking friends with 50 million dollar businesses, just what's in the Billy the Kid case for them. Self-styled Deputy Steve Sederwall's Mayor's Report of May 2003, may be the answer. "I know it is a crazy idea but won't it be fun?

Sandy Paul and granddaughter Lyndsey Hall, who vowed to chain herself to the gate of the cage guarding Bill's grave if anyone came to dig him up. She said she'd charge child abuse if they tried to remove her.

24

TWO COURAGEOUS TOWNS

(Published September 17, 2004)

Add up three sheriffs, one governor, and a $50 million a year law firm and you get power with a big "P." Or a giant with a big "G," as in Goliath.

Add up in opposition, the little village of Fort Sumner plus the little town of Silver City and you have courage with a big "C" or determination with a big "D," as in David. And it all spells out the Billy the Kid case.

For the past year, these two economically depressed communities have stood up to the relentless onslaught of frivolous litigation to get at the bones of Billy and his mother. Their saga is a tale of challenged citizens uniting in a common cause.

Forced to use the limited time resources of their elected officials and overburdened courts, they also had to live with the risk of economic retaliation. Some reported threats that "You can't stop us. We're backed by the governor and the biggest lawyers."

Since we are about to have a big showdown on September 27 when the Billy the Kid Case will be heard in district court in Fort Sumner, let's take a closer look at the protagonists.

The Village of Fort Sumner with 1200 residents, a budget of about $650,000 and a per capita income of about $13,000, relies on tourists for approximately half its revenues. That means visitors from over the country and world coming to the Billy the Kid grave. More profoundly, many of the residents are natives. The Billy the Kid heritage is part of their identity, like their own family histories.

To give you a feel, one bright twelve year old said she would chain herself to the grave if they tried to get at it, so they would be charged with child abuse. Mayor Raymond Lopez is not only standing for his town, but was selling cupcakes to raise money for its Billy the Kid Legal Defense Fund.

The town of Silver City, with 10,000 residents, a budget of about $7 million and a per capita income of about $18,500 has had an even more grim experience. From October 2003 to January of this year it has had litigation involving two petitions to exhume Billy's mother–one of them brought by the governor.

Though Silver City and Grant County had supported Bill Richardson by landslide numbers in the 2002 election, he never consulted with them and never bothered to respond to their petition to back off, signed by the mayor, town councilors, head of the Chamber of Commerce and director of their museum.

One of the town councilors said, "Because of our attempt to protect the sanctity of our graves and our economic base, we have suffered Richardson's wrath."

Richardson's line-item veto of a legislative appropriation cut $250,000, which appears chillingly vindictive in that it was for the expansion of Memory Lane Cemetery, where Billy's mother is buried. Only 60 plots remain. And as a touching note, there are always flowers left by tourists on her grave.

On December 1, 2003, Governor Richardson stated on KOB TV that he wanted DNA from Billy and his mother, even though his own Office of the Medical Investigator had already refused exhumation, saying it was valueless.

Was it coincidence that he decided to weigh in just seven days before the Silver City court was to hear the case for digging up Billy's mother? And was it coincidence that the judge kicked that political football to Fort Sumner for it to worry about?

Governor Richardson has tried to steamroll Grant and De Baca county district courts, has backed the three sheriffs in a case which seems to be using taxpayer money for personal gain, has refused to stop despite the pleas of elected officials, and has punished the communities for defending themselves.

Richardson talks about pardoning Billy. Maybe Billy should pardon him. Everyone knows the outcome of the first David and Goliath and many are hoping history will repeat itself.

And in modern times we don't use slingshots. We vote.

25

BILLY'S PARDON

(Published September 19, 2004)

Governor Bill Richardson says the reason he got himself involved in the Billy the Kid case is that he needs to decide whether to pardon Billy.

Among the governor and the three sheriffs, there is a list of reasons, almost as long as the list of Billy's alleged victims, about why they are in this case.

It is an official criminal investigation, an effort to find out who Pat Garrett killed in Fort Sumner, an effort to clear his name, an effort to learn what happened in the Lincoln County Court House when two deputies were shot and Billy escaped, an effort to promote tourism, an effort to dig up Billy and his mom to find matching DNA, an effort to prove Brushy Bill and other pretenders are fakes and an effort to decide whether to pardon Billy.

So far, the case has focused on digging up Billy and his mother for their DNA. The quest hit high center when the state Office of the Medical Investigator said the search would be valueless. So the sheriffs and governor trotted off to court to find a judge who would overrule DNA experts on their subject of expertise. That has taken nine months and stretched the budgets of Silver City and Fort Sumner to the breaking point.

During that time, Governor Richardson has insisted he wants the DNA even though it has nothing to do with pardoning Billy.

Here's the story on Billy's pardon. In 1879, Governor Lew Wallace seems to have promised Billy a pardon for his Lincoln County War-related murders. The victims were Lincoln County Sheriff William Brady, his deputy George Hindman, and bounty-hunting farmer Buckshot Roberts.

In exchange, Billy would testify to a grand jury about the murder of attorney Huston Chapman to which he was a witness. Billy testified but the governor didn't hold up his end of the deal. Billy wrote many eloquent letters from prison pleading with the governor to live up to his word.

The pardon never came. The reason for Wallace's inaction is unclear, but it has nothing to do with whom Garret shot three years later, and certainly nothing to do with anyone's DNA.

When Governor Richardson announced his support of the sheriffs' case more than a year ago, there was no talk of grave-digging. The governor talked of a series of hearings in Billy the Kid historic sites around the state.

That possibility is still open. Experts in history and law could conduct debates or mock trials designed to reveal the various pressures and considerations weighing upon Governor Wallace's decision to do nothing. Those many pressures would provide a good overview for the public of the multi-faceted Lincoln County War.

But instead, Governor Richardson has allowed himself to be drug along by the sheriffs in their misguided tangle of contradictions and trashistory. He has appointed a lawyer to channel Billy's purported desire to be dug up along with his mother. The lawyer has been helping the sheriffs in their efforts even though those efforts have nothing to do with whether Billy should be granted a pardon or not.

It is downright inspiring that our governor would take time out of his schedule to help a spirit in need. Apparently his motive is increased tourism, but the controversy over whether Billy and his mother really are buried in Fort Sumner and Silver City hasn't helped tourism in those communities, according to local businesses and a state Tourism Department report.

And if bodies are exhumed and no matching DNA is found, as the Office of the Medical Investigator predicts, the effect on those communities will be considerable, especially on Fort Sumner. And that is in addition to the money they already have had to spend to defend their municipal cemeteries on behalf of families with relatives in nearby plots.

So let's get on with investigating a pardon and forget about court action. Billy's pardon has nothing to do with Billy's bones.

Fort Sumner Mayor Raymond Lopez wearing "silver" bolo replacement and carrying a tray of cupcakes from a bake sale that raised money to defend the village of Fort Sumner in court action to dig up Billy.

26

THE GOLDEN BOLO

(Published September 20, 2004)

Something strange happened when Governor Richardson visited Silver City on September 8. He told the officials there that they "had nothing to worry about" when it came to the grave of Catherine Antrim, mother of Billy the Kid in their Memory Lane Cemetery. There are several reasons why that statement is strange.

First, he was referring to the Billy the Kid case, which is a murder investigation by the sheriffs of Lincoln and De Baca Counties and a supposedly deputized mayor. The case involves their year-long attempt to get at her bones. How can a governor control the outcome of a criminal case enough to tell officials "not to worry?"

Second, Silver City has plenty of reasons to worry. As many know, the governor joined the Billy the Kid case himself last November by bringing in Bill Robins, a high powered Texas attorney friend of his to speak for the dead Billy the Kid and say he wanted his mother dug up. Since the dead don't speak in court, the governor had already given Silver City a taste of his operating style.

Third, Silver City officials fought back and refused to be steamrolled by that juggernaut of executive power. The grave was not violated for the governor's publicity stunt. And in a result which appears undeniably connected, this year the governor line-item vetoed the $250,000 which the legislature had already approved for desperately needed expansion of Memory Lane Cemetery.

Fourth, it was recently reported that Richardson's Texas lawyer is still on the loose in New Mexico. He appears tired of speaking for the dead, since it was announced on August 12 that he would be representing the three live sheriffs. They plan to return to Silver City if their forensic expert, paid for by the History Channel, finds DNA on an old carpenter's bench on which dead Billy may have laid.

Meanwhile, there is even more action in the other battleground of the Billy the Kid case–Fort Sumner, the site of Billy's grave and the current target of these DNA-crazed investigators. On October 1 of last year Governor Richardson visited and told Mayor Raymond Lopez he "had nothing to worry about that grave." It happens that Mayor Lopez was all dressed up for the visit, wearing a limited edition bolo with a golden figure of Billy which was so realistic that the cartridges in his gun belt and the trigger on his Winchester carbine were visible.

A New Mexico artist had made the figures as tokens of appreciation for those opposing the Billy the Kid caper and as a symbol of their solidarity in protecting the history of Billy the Kid and its historic sites. Because of a foundry fluke three figures had turned golden. That was one.

It caught the eye of the highest executive in the state. He asked for it. Mayor Lopez said, "I'll give it to you if you give your word that you'll protect Fort Sumner from the case." The governor did and walked off with the golden bolo.

On February 24 of this year, Richardson's attorney, Bill Robins, filed in the De Baca County District Court to get at Billy's bones.

And not only was dead Billy a petitioner with the three sheriffs, but outrageously, he was the ONLY petitioner in a document to remove respected Judge Ricky Purcell.

And now on September 27, Fort Sumner will be fighting for its economic life in that court, as attorneys will present motions to dismiss the ill-advised case. And to raise money for the legal defense, Mayor Lopez had to sell cupcakes.

Of course Mayor Lopez wants that golden bolo back. And for the artist it has become a symbol of broken faith and abuse of power.

So remember, if Governor Richardson says, "You have nothing to worry about," start worrying.

27

KID CASE REALLY ABOUT GARRETT

(Published September 22, 2004)

The ironic twist to the Billy the Kid case is that it's not really about Billy. It's all about Sheriff Pat Garrett. According to the three sheriffs, their quest to dig up Billy and his mother began as an effort to prove that Garrett shot Billy and, therefore, Brushy Bill, et. al. were fakes and Garrett was a true hero.

The trouble is that nearly everyone already knew that. Practically the entire town of Fort Sumner filed past Billy's body on the carpenter's workbench that night and the next day. Billy was well-known in the community, so it would quickly have become evident if the body had been someone else's.

So it became necessary to convince the public that over a century of investigative work by respected historians may have been wrong. And that made Garrett the criminal in the official criminal investigation brought by the sheriffs.

So suddenly our hero became the suspect in a conspiracy with his supposed friend Billy to kill an innocent man to substitute for the Kid. And Garrett is also implicated in helping Billy escape from the Lincoln County Courthouse two months earlier by supplying a gun he used while killing Garrett's two deputies.

Billy was pulled into the case because he is an international celebrity, whose name immediately causes the media to take notice. Digging up graves is also a real attention grabber. And so is DNA, the new scientific tool that solves everything.

That doesn't include 123-year-old murder cases, but who's to know the difference? Unfortunately for the sheriffs and governor, the state Office of the Medical Investigator knew the difference and that's why the case had to go to court.

The most credible living source on Pat Garrett is Leon Metz, Garrett's famous biographer. Metz says, "There is no question in my mind that Garrett shot and killed Billy the Kid. A claim to the contrary is preposterous. Besides the irrefutable evidence of identification of the body, Garrett was a very proud man, who could not have lived with that lie."

And as to the friendship motive for murder claimed in the Billy the Kid Case, Metz says, "I can say there exists no trace of evidence that they were friends. At best they may have been acquainted in 1878 when both lived in Fort Sumner."

Among the many holes in this Swiss cheese case is the question of motive. Facts show that prior to nailing the Kid on July 14, 1881, Pat had two other chances. On December 19, 1880, he and his posse ambushed Billy and pals in Fort Sumner and killed Tom O'Folliard. Three days later at Stinking Springs he killed Charlie Bowdre thinking he was Billy because he walked out of the rock house wearing Billy's distinctive sombrero. That's not how friends treat friends.

Though the three sheriffs are willing to dig up graves to find DNA in their "search for the truth," there is plenty of Garrett DNA still walking around.

In an affidavit attached to their "criminal investigation" a man swears that Garrett's widow told him in 1940 when he was a boy that Garrett had not killed the Kid. Unfortunately she died in 1936. So the question is why didn't they question a real live Garrett? The answer may be their unique investigative style of avoiding anything that disagrees with what they want to find.

Since Governor Richardson was considerate enough to provide a lawyer to speak for dead Billy, maybe we should put the word out that Pat needs one too, so he can sue the sheriffs for defamation of his character.

So a case that began as an amorphous effort to clear the good name of the patron saint of Lincoln County sheriffs, reveal the hoaxters trying to be Billy, increase tourism and get a few people their 15 minutes of fame, has now become a hoax itself.

Lincoln County Commissioner Leo Martinez honored by Fort Sumner Mayor Raymond Lopez for questioning whether Lincoln County money was used to go after Billy's bones.

28

SOME GOOD COMES FROM BAD

(Published September 26, 2004)

People in the intellectual community as well as fans of Billy the Kid and Pat Garrett in this country and around the world have responded to the Billy the Kid case filed by the three sheriffs with gratifying strength and unity.

Like an old-fashioned case of chicken pox, once it's over, it leaves you tougher because you developed an immunity. Good things can come from bad.

The Billy the Kid case is said to have begun when the three sheriffs took a trail ride or tipped a few drinks together, or both. What has been so bothersome to its observers over the past year is that something as ridiculous and consuming of public officials' time and resources was allowed to go on so long. And if that wasn't bad enough, it seems from the conclusions of experts in history, science, and the law that there was an effort to hoodwink us. It really was The Lincoln County Hoax.

For over a year, the sheriffs had Governor Bill Richardson in the saddle with them. He recently has thought better of it and has withdrawn his support. He says he was interested only in the tourism value of it, but never suspected the opposition it would receive from Silver City and Fort Sumner. But the attorney Richardson appointed for Billy still is in the case representing the sheriffs.

People have resented being treated like suckers, worrying that officials are taking a free ride with their tax dollars, and realizing that "solving" an already solved murder 123 years old has higher priority in Lincoln and De Baca County law enforcement than solving real murders for bereaved families.

And what was the result? First, nobody was taken in. The three sheriffs have been scooting between Silver City and Fort Sumner trying to sell their tale to courts and trying to get at the bones of Billy and his mother.

But so far no one is biting. Not a single expert, other than forensic specialist Dr. Henry Lee (being paid by the History Channel and of O.J. Simpson defense fame) has done anything but laugh or get outraged.

Secondly, we started to look closer at the perpetrators. Sheriff Graves is facing recall. Deputy Sheriff Sederwall now shows no sign of being a real deputy. Sheriff Sullivan is clinging to the hope that by saying he is conducting a real criminal investigation, he can shield his departmental finances from public scrutiny. And the governor's attorney is still talking to dead Billy.

Meanwhile back in the real world, the communities of Fort Sumner and Silver City have taken another look at their heritage of historic sites, visited and cherished by tourists from around the world. And they have found pride, which has united not only the townspeople, but has brought together the towns.

On September 27 in Fort Sumner, when the judge will hear the motions to dismiss the Billy the Kid case, Mayor Terry Fortenberry of Silver City will be there to show solidarity with Mayor Raymond Lopez, standing for Fort Sumner. And last year Mayor Lopez did the same for Fortenberry.

In fact the people coming to bolster the opposition prove that good can come from bad. Frederick Nolan, the world's expert on Lincoln County War history will be there from England. Leon Metz, Garrett's famous biographer, will come from Texas. Shared economic goals brings Cissy McAndrew, executive director of the Silver City Chamber of Commerce. Lincoln County Commissioner Leo Martinez is coming too in an effort to heal any rift between Lincoln and De Baca counties.

In fact, the whole thing makes me proud. People have been talking for years about a Billy the Kid and Pat Garrett historic trail that would circle through our state and join the towns that were a part of their history.

That includes Silver City, of Billy's childhood and his mother's grave, Santa Fe where he was in jail, Old Mesilla where he stood trial, Lincoln where he had his great escape, and Fort Sumner where he and Pat had their fateful showdown and where Billy is buried.

Maybe that trail ride that took a wrong turn could put New Mexicans back on the trail of their unmatchable history of the Old West and its historic sites.

Historian Frederick Nolan came from England for the big Victory Party.

29

VICTORY IN FORT SUMNER

(Published October 1, 2004)

Instead of a court hearing, Fort Sumner held a victory celebration on Sept. 27 to mark the dismissal of proceedings to exhume Billy the Kid.

Three days earlier, attorneys for the sheriffs agreed to dismissal of the case, with prejudice, meaning it can't be refiled. Fort Sumner officials consider it a total victory, ending the effort to dig up Billy's bones.

A big party was held at City Hall, complete with a banquet of cold cuts, fruit punch and chocolate chip cookies. It doesn't get much better than that.

Beforehand, Mayor Raymond Lopez presented certificates of honorary citizenship in the Village of Fort Sumner to visiting dignitaries from as far away as England. The world's preeminent authority on the Lincoln County War, Frederick Nolan, of Chalfont, St. Giles, England, made a special trip for the event.

Also present were Silver City Mayor Terry Fortenberry and Chamber of Commerce executive director Cissy McAndrew. Last January Fort Sumner officials attended Catherine Antrim's exhumation hearing in Silver City. Since then, the two communities have provided mutual support to each other in a joint effort to protect their cemeteries and tourism produced by the Billy the Kid and Pat Garrett history and legend.

Following the banquet lunch, participants made the five-mile trip south to Billy's gravesite, where Nolan placed a bouquet of flowers in front of the gravestone of Billy and his pals, Tom O'Folliard and Charlie Bowdre. Nolan declared the day a victory for truth.

Adam Baker, lead attorney for the Village of Fort Sumner, stated that he is not sure why attorneys for the sheriffs were willing to dismiss the case with prejudice. But there are some telltale signs that the battle may not be over.

The sheriffs are declining to comment about whether they plan to renew their attempt to retrieve DNA from the remains of Billy's mother, whose grave is in Silver City.

But Governor Bill Richardson has been more forthcoming. It is time the truth is known now that DNA technology is available, said Richardson spokesman Billy Sparks, following dismissal of the Fort Sumner court case. Richardson has consistently maintained that he wants "that DNA" even though his own Office of the Medical Investigator has filed legal papers saying DNA from Catherine Antrim is useless since the location of her remains is uncertain.

"I have a sinking feeling that we haven't heard the last from these three sheriffs," Baker says. He notes that Henry Lee, a forensic expert who is working with the sheriffs, has recovered some samples from a bench said to be stained with Billy the Kid's blood.

Baker speculates that legal action in Silver City focusing on the Kid's mother may be renewed soon. This should create some fire works since forensic experts around the nation acknowledge Lee's claims can never be substantiated.

Another reason the sheriffs may have backed off the dig for Billy's bones was a spirited attack against the two sheriffs from Lincoln County by County Commissioner Leo Martinez three nights before the sheriffs threw in the towel on the Fort Sumner case.

At a commission meeting, Martinez demanded that Sheriff Tom Sullivan immediately cease his investigation of the 123 year old murders and concentrate on more recent murders that remain unsolved.

A lengthy and heated discussion ensued over how much public money was used for the investigation, the origin of the private money used, whether Capitan Mayor Steve Sederwall's "reserve deputy" status qualified him to sign legal documents that are part of the investigation and whether the county is liable for their actions.

Next door in DeBaca County, Sheriff Gary Graves is having to defend himself against recall charges that include failing to maintain proper records relating to this case and others. Representing Graves against the recall is attorney Bill Robins, the lawyer Bill Richardson brought into the case a year ago to represent (and speak for) dead Billy.

More on this later.

30

TIP OF THE ICEBERG

(Published October 4, 2004)

Like an iceberg, the Billy the Kid case may be just the tip of more strange political and legal maneuverings in the state.

The case is a criminal investigation into murder initiated in Lincoln County by Sheriff Tom Sullivan, who said he deputized Capitan Mayor Steve Sederwall to help him out. Then De Baca County Sheriff Gary Graves was recruited. That added up to considerable fire power to apprehend the dead murderer, Pat Garrett, for the supposed crime of blasting away someone other than the Kid. Lincoln County Commissioner Leo Martinez recently played spoil-sport by pointing out that Lincoln County had real murders that needed to be solved.

What has astounded people for the past year is that something this absurd and so consuming of resources of public officials in Lincoln, Grant, and De Baca Counties is still living and breathing.

The reason for this eternal life is that whenever the case starts to die a natural death, two Bills step in to resuscitate it. Governor Bill Richardson keeps adding Houston, Texas, Attorney Bill Robins, partner in a $50 million a year law firm and one of the big contributors to his election campaign.

Robins' original claim to odd fame, occurred last November when he was brought into the case when the attempt to dig up

Billy's mother's bones in Silver City ran into trouble because it was opposed historically, legally, and forensically.

Unfazed by these hurdles of truth, he took seriously the claim of this being the Land of Enchantment, and began speaking for dead Billy as his "client," saying Billy wanted his mother dug up.

Arguably, this put the judge's life at risk, since he might have died laughing, but he saved himself by telling the bizarre group of one governor, a dead Billy, and three sheriffs to go to Fort Sumner after Billy's bones to see what they found there.

On September 24, they gave up in Fort Sumner, realizing that even more obstacles existed. The opposing attorneys told them bluntly that dead Billy did not exist. It also appeared that Deputy Sederwall did not exist either, as a deputy at least. Also the case did not exist, since a criminal investigation needed a criminal and Garrett did not exist.

With no case, there was no right for law enforcement officers to be there as petitioners. That took care of Sullivan and Graves. You might have thought they would all slink back to their regular jobs. But no such luck.

It is now evident that Billy's ghost may not be the only recipient of these two good Samaritan Bills. In August, forensic expert Dr. Henry Lee was hired to scrape an old table to find DNA to match with Billy's mother. Though other forensic DNA experts called the notion absurd, it was reported that trusty Attorney Bill Robins was prepared to take that "evidence" back to Silver City for the sheriffs to once again attempt to dig up Billy's mother's bones.

In September, a group of De Baca County citizens filed to recall Sheriff Gary Graves. He hadn't endeared himself by signing onto the Billy the Kid case. Even he admitted that finding no DNA "could dry up a major source of tourism revenue for Fort Sumner."

His arrest of only three DWI suspects in over two years in office also didn't help. Things looked bleak until who should appear to represent him but high-powered attorney Bill Robins.

Immediately after the Fort Sumner Billy the Kid case withdrawal, Governor Richardson went on television, saying the case would be continued. A pattern is emerging, and it isn't that everyone is named Bill. Why are these two big Bills so interested in little Billy?

Should we worry about what's behind this, or are we just witnessing the bulldog tenacity of a successful politician and a successful trial lawyer? Time will tell, because they are not shy about leaving tracks.

31

BILLY AND JACKIE

(Published January 3, 2005)

News reports about the lawsuits over Jackie Spencer's estate are exceeding the coverage of the Dow Jones heiress' death in May 2003. They rekindle memories of her influence on Lincoln County politics and remind us of recent Lincoln County maneuverings.

Spencer and her husband Hugh Bancroft, Jr. moved to New Mexico in 1948, after he purchased a ranch near Capitan. Jackie had three children during the next five years. When her husband died in 1953, Jackie became the beneficiary of a very large estate, now valued at over $50 million.

The following year, she married Dr. A.N. Spencer, a Carrizozo physician. Jackie Spencer quickly became involved in charitable projects in the area. She built a community center and a golf course in Carrizozo and she sponsored ski programs for students from area school districts.

Her philanthropy was appreciated, but public officials say it came with strings. Although she had given her money to public bodies, she wanted a say in how it was spent.

That got her in many battles with town councils and school boards, which noted that when her money became a part of public funds, elected public officials would decide how it was spent. It also meant her money must be accounted for in local government budgets.

Fast forward a half-century to 2004, when three sheriffs from the area conducted a criminal investigation into whether Pat Garrett shot Billy the Kid and how Billy got the gun with which he shot the first deputy sheriff in the Lincoln County Courthouse.

A fair amount of money appeared to be spent on the official investigation, but not out of public coffers. When public officials asked where the money was coming from, the sheriffs said it was private money so it didn't have to be revealed.

This case differed from the Spencer situation because she gave her money to a public body, likely for tax purposes, and then wanted some control over how it was spent. The private money used by the sheriffs didn't come from checks written to a public body, thus they contended, it didn't have to be reported or tracked.

It seemed to me there was a need for more sunshine on the process. But the sheriffs stuck to their guns and the attorney general was of no help in clarifying the situation.

Possibly what the sheriffs did was technically legal. But it still bothers me that an official criminal investigation can be conducted totally with private money. That was the sort of thing that happened in Billy the Kid's time, when the Santa Fe Ring, a cabal of lawyers, politicians, judges and law enforcement officers ran the state, including Lincoln County.

Or maybe this was just a fun thing the sheriffs had going on the side. Maybe they just wanted to help tourism in the area and get a little notoriety for themselves. They did succeed in getting a History Channel program produced on Billy, although its main theme seemed to be to question the circumstances of his death and burial.

Silver City is now promoting the Billy legend, which it never did before. The sheriffs say tourism has increased in Billy the Kid Country, but a state Tourism Department study disagrees. And Lincoln's Wortley Hotel, as we reported recently, has closed.

The effort to dig up Billy and his mother for a DNA match was misguided. DNA science can't handle remains that old. A failure would have put in doubt the Fort Sumner and Silver City grave sites and shot a hole in the Billy legend.

A public poll by True West magazine showed respondents favoring exhumation, but the towns of Fort Sumner and Silver City had to fight it. They own the cemeteries and history is on their side.

That's not to say everyone in Fort Sumner and Silver City opposed exhumation. A few weeks after Fort Sumner officials presented Billy the Kid bolo ties to the leaders of the anti-exhumation movement, the three sheriffs were presented with Billy belt buckles, reportedly by someone in Fort Sumner.

Lincoln County Deputy Sheriff Steve Sederwall, Lincoln County Sheriff Tom Sullivan and De Baca County Sheriff Gary Graves display belt buckles presented to them by an admirer. Old Lincoln County Courthouse is in the background.

EPILOGUE

Billy the Kid's life was short, but his legend continues to add more chapters. This was the latest, but by no means the final chapter. The court victory in Fort Sumner closed this one, but there are sure to be many more.

Governor Bill Richardson has withdrawn his effort to obtain DNA from the remains of Billy and his mother, but at least two of the three sheriffs continue their interest, although in different capacities. Sullivan's term as Lincoln County sheriff ended December 31, 2004. Sederwall still is mayor of Capitan but no longer is affiliated with the Lincoln County sheriff's office.

Reports circulate about the sheriffs' involvement in foreign films about Billy. The district court judge in Silver City has not completely closed the door on digging up Billy's mother, Catherine Antrim. The forensic scientist recruited by the sheriffs to find some of Billy's DNA from historical objects has not reported on his laboratory results. And the sheriffs have an agreement with Governor Bill Richardson to make a recommendation about whether to issue the pardon for Billy that Governor Lew Wallace had promised in 1881.

As additional chapters unfold, updated editions of this book will be published. One positive outcome of the past two year's excitement is that there has been more digging into history. Both the Discovery and History channels have produced updates, one of which raised the possibility that Billy produced some living, walking DNA. And there even are some hints about where that descendent might be found.

More action could start at any time. Billy may ride one more time. But for now it appears that you can keep a bad man down.

Wortley Hotel in Lincoln, before the 2004 Billy the Kid Trail Ride.

POSTSCRIPTS

WORTLEY HOTEL FOR SALE

(Exactly as published December 26, 2004)

The historic Wortley Hotel in Lincoln, N.M. is on the market again. Owner Tim Hagaman hasn't had the financial resources to do the fix-up and promotion the old hotel needs to stay in business.

It isn't for lack of interest about what the hotel means to the community and the Billy the Kid legend. Hagaman is a historian who has decorated the restaurant's walls with his personal collection of old maps, newspapers and paintings. And he gives tours of Lincoln and lectures about the Lincoln County War.

The hotel has seven guest rooms, decorated as they were over 100 years ago, including brass beds and kiva fireplaces. The restaurant is a popular place when it is open.

In May of 2003, when I wrote my first column about efforts by Sheriffs Tom Sullivan, Steve Sederwall and Gary Graves to look into aspects of the Billy the Kid legend, I mentioned that it would be great if their activities renewed enough interest in the Kid to get the Wortley opened again.

That casual comment brought a torrent of reader responses from Lincoln County residents letting me know that the Wortley most certainly was open and how could I make such a horrible mistake.

I now know that for several years the Wortley had been opening on April 28 to commemorate the 1881 escape of Billy the Kid from the Lincoln County Courthouse just down the street.

The Wortley was where Deputy Sheriff Bob Olinger was having lunch with his prisoners on that day, when he heard shots from the courthouse and rushed to see what had happened.

That was Olinger's last meal because Billy was waiting for him with Olinger's own shotgun. He emptied both barrels just as Olinger looked up to see the Kid standing in a second-floor window.

The Wortley was built in 1872. It burned down once or twice, but kept being rebuilt. The original hotel housed workers who were building "Murphy's Big Store" down the street. The imposing two-story adobe soon became the courthouse.

In 1878, the Wortley was taken over as the headquarters for Sheriff Peppin and his deputies during the famous "Five Day Battle" of the Lincoln County War. Later, during court sessions, it housed judges, lawyers, law men and other official visitors. For awhile, Sheriff Pat Garrett owned the hotel.

Although the Wortley has opened on April 28 for the past several years, it has closed on October 15 each year. During the off-season, it would open for special events, such as small conferences, private parties, wedding receptions and family reunions.

The Wortley Restaurant, named for its first cook, Sam Wortley, is often packed when it is open. It has been popular with people all over the county because of its ambience and good food.

One of the specials is pot roast and mashed potatoes, the meal Olinger didn't quite finish on the day he died. And there's even a figure of Olinger sitting at one of the tables.

Along the front of the hotel is a 92-foot porch, perfect for relaxing in a rocking chair and enjoying the quiet and beauty of the surrounding hills or for visiting with other guests.

With the interest in Billy the Kid that has been stirred up the past two years, the Wortley should be a nice investment for someone with the good of the town at heart and the resources to restore the building.

Those interested in more information about the Wortley can go to the Billy the Kid Outlaw Gang Web site at www.BTKOG.com.

New Mexico Govornor Bill Richardson promoting the 2005 Billy the Kid Trail Ride.

RETRACE BILLY'S LAST RIDE

(Exactly as published January 12, 2005)

Do you know it is still possible to retrace Billy the Kid's last trail ride from Lincoln to Fort Sumner?

There are many more fences now than there were in Billy's day, but once a year, ranchers along that trail, not only to open their gates, but they feed, entertain and put riders up for the night.

The 125-mile ride, lasting seven days, begins on April 28, the day Billy escaped from the Lincoln County jail in 1881 and headed for Fort Sumner, where he had many friends. Along the way, friendly ranchers took good care of him, as they now do for the trail riders.

This will be the fourth year for the trail ride. Nineteen riders participated in the entire ride last year, with day riders pushing the total up to 25 or so.

The adventure is coordinated by New Mexico State University's Rural Economic Development Through Tourism project, which is a part of the Cooperative Extension Service of the NMSU Department of Agriculture. Rex Buchman, the extension agent in Fort Sumner, is the ramrod of the operation.

The journey begins at the Wortley Hotel with an evening meal of pot roast and mashed potatoes, the meal Deputy Bob Olinger was eating when he heard shots from the courthouse across the street and ran to see what was happening.

This time, everyone gets to finish their meal before going outside to witness a reenactment of Billy's famous escape by the Lincoln County Sheriff's Posse. Participants also can take a guided tour of Lincoln, led by Wortley hotel owner Tim Hagaman, who along with Buchman hatched the idea of an annual trail ride in 2002 and scouted the trail.

This year's ride will be held April 27 to May 5, 2005. It begins with check-in at the Pageant Grounds and a night at the Wortley across the street. Then on April 28th, the 124th anniversary of Billy's escape, riders will head up over Capitan Gap for a week of trekking through mountains, high desert grasslands and across the Pecos River.

Riders will stay at ranch camps, where they will learn the history of Billy the Kid, share stories around campfires under starry skies and build memories to last a lifetime.

The ride is billed as a "Wild at Heart" sort of adventure. Participants are warned that there are elements of endurance on the ride. But there will always be a "cowboy taxi service" available to transport gear from camp to camp and to rescue tired travelers–man or beast.

Last year, only seven of the core 19 riders made the entire ride on horseback. One of those seven was Ollie Reed, a reporter for the Albuquerque Tribune, who wrote about his adventure.

REDTT, the sponsor of the trail ride was established in 1992 by a group headed by former U.S. Rep Joe Skeen. Its purpose is to boost rural tourism development. Three of the participating counties are Lincoln, Chaves and DeBaca, through which Billy's last trail ride wanders. Another sponsor, the Billy the Kid Outlaw Gang also has taken an interest in promoting rural tourism throughout Billy the Kid Country.

The price for the entire package is $1250, which includes food, lodging and entertainment. If you just want to join in for a day or so, the cost is $150 per day, plus a $50 one-time fee. The trail ride coordinator is Wally Roberts, 10600 Monarch, Hobbs, NM 88242.

Or check the website: www.billythekidtrailride.com.

A few months later, the Outlaw Gang hosts a campout north of Ruidoso at the approximate date of Billy's death on July 14, 1881. This year's campout will be held July 21-25 at the Cedar Creek Campground, campsite #2, in Ruidoso. The campout features food, games, speakers, entertainment, contests and lots of storytelling. The cost is $10 for each vehicle.

We'll tell you more about the campout once the trail ride is over.

NASCAR BILLY

(Exactly as published February 28, 2005)

Folks in southern New Mexico are upset again with the "Governor of Albuquerque" as many down there call Governor Bill Richardson.

This time it is over the almost simultaneous decisions not to accept the offer of a Western museum in Ruidoso Downs and six recently-restored buildings in Lincoln, while announcing a proposal to help fund the privately-owned Unser Racing Museum in Albuquerque.

Both are worthy projects. Both would promote tourism. And both are unrelated. It isn't an either/or situation. It's just that the decisions were made very close to each other and both involved a figure of $800,000.

That's how much the state figures the Wild West properties would cost the state in operational funds each year and the amount of capital outlay funds proposed to donate to the racing museum.

So taking over the big Hubbard Museum of the American West and half the town of Lincoln would have been a much bigger expenditure in the long run. But they are a big part of New Mexico's history and a big tourist draw, both being associated with New Mexico's best-known personality, Billy the Kid.

Hubbard's Western museum began as the Museum of the Horse, and not in the Ruidoso area. We have visited the spot in

Patagonia, Arizona, where it began. That building was empty at the time we visited, but the Big Steer Saloon across the parking lot was still much fun.

The state already owns many of the historic buildings in the town of Lincoln and Hubbard owns most of the rest. Having the entire town as a state monument is a dream of many in the area, and the possibility of it happening had the museum employee we talked with at the old Lincoln County Court House last summer very excited.

R.D. Hubbard has done much to develop Lincoln County in the past several years. He owns Ruidoso Downs and the Billy the Kid Casino next door to the museum and is a part owner of the new Hobbs horse track and casino. His offer was generous but did not include an endowment sufficient to continue the 26 employees and upgrade the museum to American Association of Museum standards.

The Unsers' auto racing museum in Albuquerque also will be a tourist draw. Indianapolis, the town that made them famous, wanted it, but the Unsers, who have done their bit for Indianapolis over the years, are New Mexico through and through.

In the early 1960s, we joined my parents at Speedway Park in Albuquerque to watch Bobby and Al race old stock cars and knock the slowpokes off the track. They didn't lose very often and it was wise to stay out of their way. They were scrappers and had grown up that way.

Stories abound about their fights with each other at the Unser garages on Central Ave. atop the West Mesa. My introduction to the Unsers occurred my freshman year at the University of New Mexico. I wheeled into a drive-in with a date, who suddenly said to keep going because we had to get out of there quickly.

No, it wasn't an old boyfriend she'd spotted. It was Bobby Unser, whom she said, she had seen beat someone mercilessly at another drive-in the previous weekend. That was good enough for me to keep moving.

Come to think of it, there is another connection between the two museums. Bobby and Al would have made excellent gunslingers a century earlier. And Billy the Kid would have been a champion race car driver. Of course, all three of them should have been driving on the NASCAR circuit, rather than the more gentlemanly open-wheel racing of Indy.

They would have made quite a threesome, whether fighting the crooked Santa Fe Ring and its Murphy-Dolan gang or driving for the top NASCAR team.

It's too bad New Mexico can't find the resources to adequately honor both.

www.ingramcontent.com/pod-product-compliance
Lightning Source LLC
Chambersburg PA
CBHW021340090426
42742CB00008B/669